# THE LIFE AND LETTERS

## OF

# EMIL AND MARIE SYWULKA

*Anna Marie Dahlquist*

*By Anna Marie Dahlquist*

Kings River Publications
1643 Winter St.
Kingsburg, CA 93631

# THE LIFE AND LETTERS OF EMIL AND MARIE SYWULKA

© 2004 by Anna Marie Dahlquist

International Standard Book Number
1-894928-50-4

Printed in the United States of America

# Contents

# Preface

Emil and Marie Sywulka were letter-writers. Many of their long, hand-written letters have been lost, but many still remain, housed now at the Billy Graham Center Archives in Wheaton, IL.

I am particularly grateful for those persons who preserved and shared Sywulka family correspondence: Emil's siblings (Julia Sywulka Blankenship and Edward and Nora Gray) and Emil and Marie's sons (Paul Emil Sywulka and Edward Frederick Sywulka.) Thanks also goes to the Moody Bible Institute and the Billy Graham Center for making their records available.

Those who critically read the manuscript and gave valuable suggestions also deserve appreciation: Edward and Pauline Sywulka, Beth Sywulka, and Dr. Paul Sywulka of Guatemala.

Thanks to those who contributed photographs, Edward Sywulka, Peggy Stoddard, Joellen Simeon and Liz Finnell.

Special thanks to Dawna Sanders for her expertise in digitalizing the photographs and to Dr. Rich Sanders for ably formatting the text.

I have taken the liberty of making minor spelling changes in the letters I quoted. For example, I changed *Kiswahili* to *Swahili*, *Kisukuma* to *Sukuma*, and *Nasa* to *Nassa*, in order to conform to modern usage. I have not, however, sought to make changes for the sake of "political correctness." Emil and Marie spoke of *natives* rather than *nationals*; for that was the common usage in their day. To them, the word *native* had no demeaning connotation. It merely designated a person of African descent who was born in Africa.

To quote every Sywulka letter in full would have made for tedious reading indeed. My hope is that the snippets I have selected will help Emil and Marie—and their faith and faithfulness—come alive for the reader.

Anna Marie Dahlquist

# CHAPTER 1
# Emil
# 1879 – 1906

## *SLOVAKIAN ROOTS*

Emil Sywulka was born on May 20, 1879, in a village called Kamienka. Still a small town today, it lies in eastern Slovakia, a land bordered on the north by Poland, on the east by the Ukraine, and on the south by Hungary. For over a thousand years, this little corner of the globe was crushed by a long series of conquerors; only in the twentieth century did it become a sovereign nation in its own right. When Emil was born, Slovakia was part of the Austro-Hungarian Empire, under the sway of Emperor Francis Joseph.

The fact that the Slovaks had no independent state of their own before 1918 may help to explain why Emil always identified himself as an Austrian, while his sister Julia called herself Hungarian, and many of his cousins referred to themselves as Czechs.

Emil was the first child of Peter and Anna (Jaromisz) Szivulka. They named him John Emanuel, after both grandfathers, but he was known simply as Emil.

## *JOURNEY TO AMERICA*

Times were hard. So Peter, a music teacher by trade, decided to emigrate. Family tradition says he left without proper exit papers. When he arrived at Hamburg, so the story goes, he showed his teacher's certificate to the unsuspecting officials, who couldn't read Slovak. They stamped it as a valid passport, and he got on the boat with his little family, bound for New York, one of countless immigrants eager to enter at that golden door.

1

The voyage took three weeks, and the family traveled "steerage," which can be defined as "any markedly inferior, overcrowded, third-class accommodation."

It was November, 1882, when the ship docked. As Peter entered the new land, his surname was mistakenly registered as *Sywulka,* and thus it has remained ever since.

### WESTWARD TO WISCONSIN

With Peter and Anna were Emil and their second child. They had just buried their third child in Slovakia a few months before. Much later, Emil's youngest sister Julia recalled what her parents told her about the journey:

> *They stopped in Pittsburgh, Pennsylvania, hoping that my father could earn enough money to buy a farm. My father worked in the mines, my mother helped by cooking and cleaning in a boarding house. My father was frail and not accustomed to labor, so could not continue that work.*
>
> *They learned about land in Wisconsin that was available at a price they could afford. They arrived in Whittlesey in the winter. Whittlesey was a German community hostile to other immigrants. Little Milchen became ill… The neighbors refused to give or sell milk to my father. They claimed they only had enough for their children. The store was [about] nine miles distant in Medford. Little Milly died. She was a beautiful, beloved child. It was a serious blow! (1)*

In rapid succession, two more daughters joined the family, but died shortly after birth. Julia continues:

> *To survive the winter, my father worked in a lumber camp cutting down trees for the industry. He spent months away from the family. My mother sewed, made clothes for people, and thus earned subsistence. The land near Whittlesey was wooded, and needed to be cleared in order to farm it. Indians appeared unexpectedly and were frightening to the family. (2)*

Farming was hard work, the winters were bitterly cold, and poverty was a wolf howling at the door.

And yet some things improved. When Emil was seven, after losing four sisters, he at last got one—little Louisa—who survived.

And the next four children—three more girls and a second son—also lived.

The new babies brought joy, but also stretched the family budget. It was hard to feed so many mouths! And so, to help the family out, Emil got work when he could as an errand boy.

**The Peter Sywulka family:**

**Back:** *Louise, Emil, Jeannette, Hattie*
**Front:** *Peter, Julia, Edward, Anna*

### CHRISTIAN EXPERIENCE

In the old country, the family was devoutly Greek Orthodox, but because they settled in a German community without an Orthodox church, they worshiped at the local Roman Catholic chapel.

The priest required contributions from all members, but Peter, who was too poor to pay his dues in cash, cut wood for the cleric instead.

Emil grew up speaking three languages: Slovak in the home, German in confirmation classes at the Catholic Church, and English at school.

Even as a small child, he was interested in Africa. He later reminisced:

*When a little fellow of eight or nine I heard my parents talk*
*about Africa and cannibals and about missionaries at the*
*dinner table. In my heart I said, "That is where I am going."*
*It was a secret kept to myself until I was almost ready to go.*
*While still going to the Roman Catholic chapel I prayed many*
*Lord's prayers that God would send me as a missionary. (3)*

A portion of a 1935 letter to his cousin Michael Sivulka summarizes Emil's personal testimony:

*I was raised a Roman Catholic (there being no Greek Catholic*
*church there at Whittlesey, Wisconsin.) At the age of 19, one*
*Sunday afternoon in May, I found the Lord in my little attic*
*bedroom through the reading of some printed literature.*
*Immediately I started a Sunday school in our own home*
*which, I believe, has borne some permanent fruit. Had some*
*persecution too. (4)*

Young Emil's zeal was apparent from the beginning; he organized a number of Sunday schools in addition to the one in his home. And his teaching had a big impact on his siblings. Eventually, his whole family left the Catholic faith and began to attend a Methodist church.

## TEACHING SCHOOL

Emil's application to the Moody Bible Institute states that he attended "common school" and then spent nine months at the Medford High School. He informed Moody that he had studied "geometry, literature and physics." (5)

At that time, apparently, Wisconsin only had two requirements for elementary school teachers: that they be at least eighteen years old and that they pass an examination. Emil passed the test, and taught school for two terms. In 1903, when he applied to Moody, he was teaching in Little Black, Wisconsin, and boarding with a man named Otto Schuster. But he came home for Christmas. His baby sister Julia recalled the following:

*Before Emil went to Moody, he taught school. At Christmas*
*time, he came home and we went out to choose a tree from our*
*own farm. We chose one that would reach the ceiling, and*
*brought it home on the sleigh. Emil set it up in the center of*
*the big room. He decorated it with gold stars, made by folding*

*gold paper, and with roses made from tissue paper, and also with paper chains made of paper of various colors. We all gathered around the tree and held hands and sang carols in German, such as "O Tannenbaum." Even though the family came from Slovakia, we didn't celebrate Christmas in the Greek Orthodox way, but rather on December 25 in the German fashion, as we had settled in a German community. (6)*

Julia also recalled the influence Emil had on his younger brothers and sisters:

*Emil was a very successful teacher. He came home on his vacations, organizing, disciplining, teaching Bible to the siblings. He organized a successful Sunday School in an adjacent community, which all of us attended. He brought self-esteem to all of us. (7)*

## MOODY BIBLE INSTITUTE

Emil's letter to his cousin Michael tells how he found out about Moody at age 23:

*I picked up a* Christian Herald. *On the front page was a picture and description of the Moody Bible Institute and I at once said, "That's where I'm going." And so I did. I spent two years there. (8)*

On his Moody application, Emil wrote that he had become a Christian "four years ago." Asked about his church membership, he said, "Was a Catholic but have not joined another church yet—prefer the Methodist." The form sent in by his landlord as part of the Moody application gives this interesting note:

*"As much as I found out he is mostly converted through the writings of Mr. David C. Cook." (9)*

Rev. S. W. Ingram, elderly pastor of the Methodist Church in Phillips, Wisconsin, conscientiously filled out a reference form. He said of Emil:

*He has done good work as a school teacher... he does much work in Young Peoples Societies and has organized and maintained a number of rural sabbath schools... he has a tendency to bluntness, that is overplain speaking, but training*

*will cure this, I know, because he has improved in this*
*somewhat already... As a speaker he has no remarkable*
*characteristics. He is simple, direct, clear and is always*
*listened to with interest. His manner is quiet, his language*
*good, his words well chosen... I know of nothing to disqualify*
*[him]. He may never make a brilliant worker, but he will be*
*persistent, command confidence, be prudent and safe. [He]*
*would need instruction in tactfulness in approaching men in*
*order to [achieve] the highest usefulness. (10)*

Emil was accepted and remained at Moody for two years, eager to learn all he could. To meet his financial needs, he relied on the $125 saved from his schoolteacher's salary and also worked as a janitor.

## THE AFRICA INLAND MISSION

While at Moody, Emil learned about the Africa Inland Mission and met some of its missionaries. Africa! He had long been praying that God would send him there. He wasted no time in requesting an application form. He wrote:

*As it is my purpose and God's will I sincerely believe, to go to*
*Africa to spread the good tidings, a friend of mine, G. Haigh*
*(going out in June) directed me to write to you.*

*My two years at the Moody Bible Institute are drawing to a*
*close and after praying over the matter I feel God wants me to*
*go in the near future.*

*I have prayed that if the call should be a mistaken one, that*
*God would effectually block the [way]. I know He will guide,*
*so if you feel led, please send me an application blank.*

*Yours truly, Emil Sywulka (11)*

The AIM was a young work—founded in Philadelphia only a few years before by a group of missionary enthusiasts that included Peter Scott, Arthur Pierson and Charles Hurlburt. As the leader of the first recruits, Scott sailed from New York to Mombasa in August, 1895. By December of the following year he was dead from fever, and by 1898 the last of the first sixteen AIM missionaries had either died or left the field.

The home council leaders could have decided to close the work down, but instead they decided to go forward. Dr. A. T. Pierson said: "Gentlemen, the hallmark of God on any work is death. God has given us that hallmark. Now is the time to go forward."

The work was not destined to die. Charles Hurlburt and his wife "amazed their friends by announcing in 1901 that they planned to take their five children, age four to twelve years, to East Africa despite the terrifying scale of missionary mortality." (12). Four new missionaries sailed with them.

Charles, a skilled promoter, kept adding missionaries to his little band. Only five years after the Hurlburts opened their Kenya work, Emil was ready to join them. The requirements were simple and the application form consisted of only one page.

On the form, Emil listed his birthplace as "Austria" but his nationality as "Slav". He summarized his schooling —somewhat meager by today's standards—as "nine months high school and two years Moody Bible Institute." And he gave his work experience as "farming and teaching."

When asked why he believed God had called him to Africa, he replied: "Because when a boy God set my face toward that field, and now when I decided for that field God gave me joy and the way is opening." (13)

The dean of men at Moody was happy to recommend Emil. He wrote:

> *I am glad to state that Mr. Sywulka has my utmost confidence as to his Christian character, fervency, and devotion... He speaks three languages... I certainly feel that although he is not brilliant, he will make a good missionary. (14)*

Emil's three languages, of course, were Slovak, German and English. In Africa he would master several more. All his life he would be known as a dogged and diligent linguist, as well as an evangelist and teacher.

Before Emil could sail for Africa, he needed to attend to a very personal matter. He was engaged to a young woman who didn't share his call. Furthermore, her parents opposed her going overseas. And yet, he was not a man to lightly break a promise. What should he do?

No doubt he prayed much about the matter, and God answered. The young woman agreed to "sacrifice their union" for the sake of the gospel, and Emil was free to pursue his calling. (15)

Today missionary candidates spend months—sometimes years—raising support before they leave for the field. And then comes formal language school! But in 1906 things were different. Emil applied in mid-February. By May, he wrote from Wisconsin to let the Home Office know how eager he was to be on his way:

> *The Lord is constantly opening doors of service for me for which I just praise Him. O the riches of His grace. When we wait patiently He inclines His ear and hears our cry. I still feel that I want to travel steerage. Pray for me. (16)*

Emil didn't even mention the words "support" or "fund-raising" although lack of money may have been what was holding him back. The AIM had determined that they would stick "to a faith position in matters of finance." Charles Hurlburt was adamant about missionaries' sharing their needs with God alone. The mission's guiding principle was: "As to the work, full information; as to funds, no solicitation." (17)

Emil agreed wholeheartedly with this viewpoint, and stuck to it during his entire missionary career. During his brief stint of speaking in churches, he never mentioned money. And four months after applying, he had his passage funds in hand.

A note on the back of his application to the AIM states that he sailed on June 21, 1906, via Hamburg on the *Kaisirin Auguste Victoria*, and that he departed from Hamburg for Africa on July 7, 1906. (18)

As the ship came within sight of Mombasa, Emil's pulse quickened. He remembered the cannibal stories told around his parents' dinner table. He thought of the tiny band of initial AIM pioneers; Peter Scott, Jacob Toole, and Tom Allen all succumbed to dread fevers while most of the others resigned due to illness or discouragement. Not without good reason, Africa was known as "the white man's grave."

And yet, God had called him here. There was work for him to do, and he was eager to do it. He was risking his very life by coming to Africa, but there could be no turning back.

**References:**

(1)  Letter from Julia Sywulka Blankenship to Anna Marie Dahlquist, January 1, 1988
(2)  *Ibid.*
(3)  Letter from Emil to Michael Sivulka, February 14, 1935
(4)  *Ibid.*
(5)  Emil Sywulka application file, Moody Bible Institute
(6)  Interview with Julia Sywulka Blankenship, 1984
(7)  Letter from Julia Sywulka Blankenship to Anna Marie Dahlquist, January 1, 1988
(8)  Letter from Emil to Michael Sivulka, February 14, 1935
(9)  Emil Sywulka application file, Moody Bible Institute
(10) *Ibid.*
(11) Letter from Emil to the AIM Home Council, January 29, 1906
(12) Anderson, Dick, *We felt like Grasshoppers*, Crossway, 1994, p. 32
(13) Emil Sywulka, application to the AIM, Feb. 16, 1906
(14) Letter from Edward Marshall to the AIM Home Council, February 7, 1906
(15) Letter from Emil to the AIM Home Council, 1906
(16) Letter from Emil to the AIM Home Council, May 25, 1906
(17) Anderson, *op. cit.,* p. 32
(18) Emil Sywulka, application to the AIM, 1906

# CHAPTER 2
## Marie
## 1873 – 1906

### *EARLY LIFE*

She was their first child—a little girl with her father's curly hair and her mother's brown eyes. The proud parents, both German immigrants, carefully recorded the following in the family Bible: "Anna Maria Schneider, gebohren den 23ten December 1873."

Her father, Adam Schneider, had come from Weisenhasel in Hesse to work on the railroad in Hazleton, Pennsylvania. Her mother, Elizabeth Wiegand, was also from Hesse, born in a village called Widershausen.

Although they named the baby Anna Maria, she came to be known simply as Marie. Only rarely did she use the initials AMS. Later three more girls were born to the family: Elizabeth, Anna Barbara, and Eliza. By 1881, the family was complete with the birth of little John Adam.

Some time later, the family moved from Pennsylvania to Akron, Ohio. Here Marie's father passed away in 1890, a victim of "malarial fever." (1) Marie was only sixteen; her siblings were even younger. Her family desperately needed her help just to pay the bills, so she began taking in washing. In later life, she recalled:

> *At home I used to get up at four o'clock, get on the water, and start washing long before breakfast. That was when I was young and strong and when I had to make my own living and help support Mother and the younger children. (2)*

10

## CHURCH BACKGROUND

The Schneiders were loyal members of a German-speaking denomination known as The Evangelical Association.

These churches sprang up as a result of the labors of one Jacob Albright. He ministered to the German people of Pennsylvania, preaching first as a Lutheran and then as a Methodist exhorter. "He used the Methodist Discipline . . . preached Methodist doctrine, and was so effective that for quite some time his followers were known as the Albrights." (3)

In 1946 the Evangelical Association merged with the Church of the United Brethren in Christ, another pietistic German denomination, also strongly Methodist in doctrine and polity. The two groups then became known as the Evangelical United Brethren Church (E.U.B). By 1968 the language and cultural barriers that separated these German-speaking churches from other Methodists were gone, and the E.U.B. merged with the Methodist Church to become the United Methodist Church.

Marie always considered the Calvary Evangelical Church—located on Coburn Street in Akron—as her home church. As a child, that was where she received religious instruction and learned the beloved old German hymns. As a young missionary, she wrote letters to her supporters there, and when on furlough she returned there time and again to present Africa's challenge. When the 1946 merger changed the church's name to Calvary E. U. B., it was still supporting her. The building later burned down, and today Calvary Evangelical Church exists no more as a separate entity.

## CALL AND TRAINING

Like Emil, Marie experienced a call to missionary service as a young woman. She often prayed with a map of the world in front of her. As she asked God for guidance as to where to serve Him, her eyes were invariably drawn to Africa. She wrote to the Mission Board of the Evangelical Church, her denomination, regarding foreign service. They replied that the only opening they had at that time was in Japan.

11

**Marie in her youth**

Marie felt firmly that God had called her to Africa, and she trusted Him to lead her to another mission. But because her family depended on her, her dream was put on hold.

She undertook a rigorous nursing course at the Philadelphia General Hospital, then returned to Akron to work as a nurse and midwife. She even assisted Mrs. Harvey Firestone—of rubber tire fame—during the births of her sons, Harvey Jr. and Russell. (4)

The busy years sped by, and still her family needed her. Marie longed to study the Bible, to give herself to Christian service, and to get out to Africa where the need was so pressing. But she was patiently learning to wait for God's time, a lesson that would stand her in good stead in Africa.

By the time Marie was thirty, she at last felt free from family duties. Her younger siblings were well established and could support themselves and their mother. Marie was now ready to begin her studies at Moody Bible Institute.

> *She had spent many years in preparation for her work. The daughter of godly, missionary-minded parents, she was forced by circumstances to postpone her formal training for the field,*

*but learned many valuable lessons while playing the role of
breadwinner. Ultimately she completed a course in nursing in
a Philadelphia hospital and graduated from the Moody Bible
Institute. (5)*

Moody's brief student records indicate the following:

*She entered Moody Bible Institute on December 28, 1903 and
left February 17, 1906. Her previous occupation was a nurse.
Her education included common schools and hospital
training. Marie was converted in childhood, and her
denomination was the Evangelical Association. Christian
work that she had done included women's and children's work
along with prison ministry. (6)*

## AFRICA INLAND MISSION

As she came to the close of her Moody training, Marie applied
to the Africa Inland Mission. About the same time, she penned the
following poem expressing her deep sense of commitment to
missionary service:

*"Called"*

*Called to shine mid heathen darkness,
God's own glory to make known,
Where through ages dark and hoary
Ne'er a beam of light has shown.*

*Called to walk among the lowly
In the way the Master trod
And by life and precept holy
Gently lead them home to God.*

*Called to tell the sweet old story,
They have waited for so long
Called to give salvation's message
Called to fill sad lives with song.*

*Called to give up all for Jesus,
Just to go where'er He sends
Knowing that His love so precious
Ever comforts and defends*

*Called, yea this my highest pleasure,*
*Just to do what He makes plain,*
*Winning man God's love to treasure*
*Through the Lamb for sinners slain*

*(7)*

By April, 1906, Marie was making the rounds of the churches of the Evangelical Association to talk about the AIM. It was now *her* mission, and she was excited about sharing its vision. She wrote to headquarters:

> *Words fail to express the joy that is mine since I know that I am really going to the land where in spirit I have been so long a time.*
>
> *I cannot understand just why God has chosen me for this work. It is enough to know that I have heard His "Go quickly and tell." I can no longer stay...*
>
> *Would it be too much to ask you to send me about 200 of those AIM folders, also about 75 Africa prayer cards. I would like these for my own church and some of the churches I am to visit—Evangelical. (8)*

### A STORMY VOYAGE

About six weeks later, Marie again wrote to the AIM headquarters, this time from the Steamship *St. Paul,* which she and two other recruits had boarded. Apparently "the Africa trio" (the names of her companions are lost to history) elected her as their secretary:

> *Greetings from the Africa trio. Well, we are actually on the way. It seems too good to be true . . . Had no trouble in New York. Got along very well indeed. Rev. Wiegand (my cousin) was here to see me off—very kind I am sure . . . We appreciated your cards so much. Just what we needed at this time. The student body and faculty of the Moody Bible Institute also remembered us. How we feel the power of their prayers.*
> *(9)*

A layover in London provided the "Africa trio" an opportunity to visit Westminster Abbey. Marie never forgot the awe she felt in that vast cathedral, nor the thrill of seeing David Livingston's grave.

The young missionaries even indulged in a shopping spree. Marie picked up some white slippers; something seemed to tell her that they might prove useful in Africa.

And then the journey continued. Violent storms tossed the ship; the entire voyage lasted forty days. (10)

## AFRICA

The travelers were glad when the ship docked at Mombasa, the Kenyan port where Peter Scott and his ill-fated band had landed eleven years earlier. Marie could hardly believe that she was actually setting foot in Africa—the land where "in spirit she had been so long."

Mombasa was bursting with tropical beauty—a riot of crimson bougainvillea bushes, purple jacaranda trees, and blue wisteria vines. Around the city were tall, dark green mango and cashew trees, large-leaved banana trees, and stately date and coconut palms.

The narrow streets of the city were full of white-robed Arabs, Indian women in silk saris, Europeans with their pith helmets, and tall tribesmen wearing next to nothing. What a fascinating melting pot of humanity!

Marie had never felt such intense, sweltering heat before, nor had she ever seen so many mosquitoes. This was the *real* Africa.

But Mombasa was not her final destination. The young missionaries set off for Nairobi, at that time a "tin town" of rusty shacks and dirty hovels. From there, a train took them up the hills to Kijabe—AIM's highland station in the heart of Kenya's Great Rift Valley. Just three years earlier Charles Hurlburt had wisely selected Kijabe as his headquarters; the city was on the railroad line and boasted both mail and telegraph service. And its higher elevation meant the missionaries would live in a cooler, more healthful climate.

The Hurlburts welcomed Marie and her companions warmly, assigning her to live in the Ladies' House and work at the station clinic.

The patients were mostly from the Kikuyu tribe. From the very first, Marie felt a deep love for them. She was especially drawn to the children who thronged the dispensary doors. Those from the mission school were clothed, but the little boys from the villages wore nothing; and the little girls wore only the scantiest of aprons. Adults sported tattered garments made of the skins of goats or oxen, along with numerous charms around their wrists and ankles.

There was so much to do! Young men suffering from snakebites or hunting wounds, young women in childbirth, children with distended stomachs and tropical maladies of many sorts. Marie was glad for her years of training and preparation; now she could put her nursing skills to good use.

She found the Kikuyu language difficult, but she accepted her linguistic limitations with good humor. She might never become a golden-tongued orator nor an able Bible translator, but she did know how to deliver babies and set broken bones. There was plenty of that kind of work to be done, and that was enough for her.

**References:**

(1)  Ohio cemetery records
(2)  Letter from Marie Sywulka to her son Edward, Sept. 18, 1933
(3)  Letter from Rev. Jim Abe of Akron to Anna Marie Dahlquist, with enclosure copied from *United Methodist Church*, p. 205
(4)  "Missionary, 90, back in Akron she left in '06." undated clipping from a 1964 Akron newspaper
(5)  *Inland Africa*, "A Jubilee of Triumph" by Nellie E. Stover, 1957
(6)  Letter from Philip Van Wynen to Anna Marie Dahlquist, July 22, 1983
(7)  Handwritten copy of 1906 poem by Marie Schneider.
(8)  Letter from Marie Schneider to the AIM, April 9, 1906
(9)  Letter from Marie Schneider to the AIM, May 19, 1906
*(10)* Akron newspaper clipping, *op. cit.*

# CHAPTER 3
## Kenya
## 1906 – 1909

**Workers at Kijabe: Emil and Marie second and third from left front**

### *KIJABE*

Charles Hurlburt was very much in charge of his mission station. His contribution, however, to the AIM work went far beyond directing the younger missionaries who gathered around him at Kijabe.

> *Charles Hurlburt defined AIM's doctrine, chiseled out its constitution, fostered two Home Councils in America and another in Britain as well as launching the work in Australia, recruited most of the 200 missionaries in place when he left, and directed the whole work with vision, care, wisdom, and authority. His gracious shadow falls on every development in AIM's first three decades (1)*

After Emil had been in Kijabe only a short time, the Hurlburts asked him "to start work high up on the misty ridges of Kikuyu country." (2) Emil was delighted. Nothing could compare with climbing the heavily forested mountains, trekking through the high country on foot, and searching out unreached villages where he could witness to his faith.

> *Someone said that Emil had "Periscopic Vision". When he*
> *was preaching on one ridge, he was always peering over the*
> *summit wondering about the needs of the people living on the*
> *other side. (3)*

## WEDDING IN A CEDAR-COVERED CHAPEL

A year after arriving in Africa, Emil was not only making periodic treks "high up on the misty ridges" of the Kikuyu territory; he was also making wedding plans.

Emil had known Marie at Moody, but at that time he'd been interested in someone else, someone who hadn't shared his missionary call. That romance, in God's providence, had come to nothing. Now he felt his heart deeply drawn to the young nurse who was just as passionate about Africa as he was.

His heart leaped for joy when she answered "yes" to his proposal of marriage. Then they set the date; their special event would take place on August 7, 1907.

Marie was nearly thirty-four; Emil was only twenty-eight, but the six-year difference mattered little to them. What mattered is that they'd be able to serve the Lord together.

**Wedding in Kijabe, August 7, 1907**

Marie, given to writing long letters full of homey details and sprinkles of humor, described the wedding in a 19-page letter to Emil's parents in Wisconsin:

*Dear Ones All:*

*I rather think that I am to be the scribe of this new firm, at least I told Emil that I would send you an account of the "event of our lives," our wedding. A man couldn't write up a wedding anyway, at least not from a woman's point of view, could he?*

*In the first place I cannot begin to tell you how much I feel your own and a part of you and all your interests. As to your last letters, well to be perfectly honest, they kind of spoiled our dinner for us. There was so much written between the lines too, that somehow touched our hearts more than we care to acknowledge. Emil while reading had to stop once in a while and choke on something that wasn't food either. My head was on his shoulder so he could not see well just how much I enjoyed your letters. Oh, we do thank you for your deep love which words cannot express. I tell dear Emil that by God's grace I want to be to him all that a wife ought to be. And by His grace I want to be to you all that a daughter ought to be.*

*Now as to the wedding. I suppose you wonder why we were married so soon. Well, in a way we both felt that this was God's time for us. In God's sight we were married anyway, so closely had our hearts been knitted together. Then too, I told Emil that during the past months (while out selecting a station) he had lived on native potatoes and corn meal long enough. I could not bear the thought of him going out alone again, living just any which way, after the manner of men. Always told me that he got along just fine. Well, maybe he did, but I venture to say that it goes better now. So we decided on Aug. 7th as our wedding day. Would like to write you all the details but can not.*

*Oh how often we said, "This wedding would be complete if only our dear ones were here—my dear husband's and mine." But of course that was out of the question. So like good children we made the best of it.*

*Well, the day dawned somewhat clouded. I kept wondering if it was going to rain although this is not the rainy season. Did not mind the sun hiding behind clouds, still wanted some sunshine, though tropical. To make a long story short the day turned out ideal. There was little hurry for much of the work had been done the day before, as decorating, cooking, etc. Still there are always enough last things to do. Most of the decorating in the chapel had been done on Tuesday, too. Here we have services at 6:30 a.m. Perhaps it was not just the proper thing to do under the circumstances but I could not help but attend the services that morning.*

*Of course I had to sit among the women from choice. In spite of myself I had to cry, for wasn't I about to leave these whom I had learned to love oh so much. Not a few of the women had been ministered to in the hour of woman's greatest trial and then, there were my precious black babies. Njoke, just behind me—perhaps the most beloved of all, and the most cunning. Interested in her from the day of her birth a little more than a year ago. Didn't I find her first tooth, help her to take her first steps, catch her smiles, let her feel my hair. Karanja at my side—black, fat, happy—also pulling at my heart strings. Well, I simply had to cry and to my credit, too, as I learned afterwards, for the women said, "Ah, she is a regular Muyikuya" (a woman of our tribe). For a Kikuyu bride is supposed to be very liberal with her tears, even weeping out loud and keeping it up until her mother-in-law says that it is enough. This may be for days or weeks.*

*They felt pleased to know that we did not like to leave them.*

*By our request, Mr. Hurlburt invited all the people who cared to, to return at 11 a.m., especially the women and children, the blowing of the cornet twenty minutes before time being the signal for their coming. Seemed rather strange to sit there and hear the invitation given and people looking at me and looking at me as they did. Emil was not present to get his share.*

*Even in the early morning the chapel looked so pretty although the decorations had not been completed. Great bowers of cedar everywhere — about the windows, doors, while the whole front was a mass of green.*

*After the services, the flowers were put in—white only—for this was a white and green wedding, so far as the church decorations went. White muslin over the pulpit platform, the place where the missionaries sat and the place where we stood. Just before we came in, muslin was also put down the aisle. This could not be done any sooner, for our black guests came unshod —a pretty clean carpet would have been ours if their dusty bare feet had passed over first.*

*We do not have a board floor in our house of worship, just the hard ground. That is one reason for putting down the muslin. The ladies did not care to soil their white dresses.*

*Well, at eleven, rather a little before, the bridegroom and bride left Mr. Hurlburt's house for the chapel, perhaps a two-minute walk. Most of the white people had preceded us. We waited just a few minutes outside for the final "get ready" inside.*

*Looking up I saw Wambui standing a little ways off. Weeping salty and bitter tears, because we were going away and she could not go with us. She is perhaps twelve years of age. For a long time, even before Emil and I had any intentions of getting married, she has called herself "our child." Don't know how I*

21

*soaped her in unless it was with bandages, for she is one of my patients. To see her weep made me sniffle too. I persuaded her to go in as the time for the ceremony had come.*

*At a given signal we started.*

*Little Grace McKenrick was our flower girl. I got her started safely at the door and she did very well for a little while or at least until two or three of the natives thought that she was in our way, that she was wandering about, not knowing just where to find a seat etc. So decided to help her and us too by pulling her aside and telling her to hurry up which she was in the point of doing. Only a quiet word to her and the well-meaning natives put things to rights. Fortunately there was no halt in our march from door to altar although Grace did not walk in a perfectly straight line, but her zig--zag journey was not her fault.*

*Emil and I came in to the strains of that beautiful song of Mendelssohn's, "Oh rest in the Lord," sung by Mrs. Divin and played by Miss Doering. Mr. Hurlburt and Mr. Riebe awaited us at the altar. After a few words by Mr. Hurlburt and a prayer by Mr. Riebe, Mr. Hurlburt spoke the words that made us husband and wife. Another prayer and all was over. Was I nervous? No, not a bit. Only I did have to use my kerchief some, but that was that black girl's fault. She got me started.*

*To the left of us, were my nursery children all in a row, with clean faces and pretty white slips on (they wear no clothes in their villages) while an old grandmother, a friend of ours, had charge of them doing her best to keep them quiet. I was surprised that they did not greet us with, "Bwana," (master) and "Bibi wa muthaiga" (lady of medicine), their name for me, but understood that they had been given orders to hold their peace. I did hear them whisper, though, and the grandmother too, rather sharply, telling them to keep still.*

*In the other Amen corner were the missionaries, music, and all that belonged to a civilized wedding. Also on this side were the girls in the station, rather young women, also here in white muslin dresses made for the great event. Back of them, the orphan boys. Back of these, the native women just as they had dropped work in garden or village. Baby either sat in mother's lap or peeped over her shoulder, for babies are carried on*

*backs here, and not in arms. The women were in native dress;
at home we would call it full dress, for arms and chest were
bare. Garments are made of skin minus the hair, are well-
greased and smoked. Dirty, oh there is no describing it.*

*On the opposite side were the men in blankets or pieces of
cloth.*

*The room was well filled, should say that there were perhaps
two hundred people there. How strange it must have seemed to
these people, this wedding of ours. The whole proceeding.
Here a man pays so many sheep or goats for a wife; then some
day, when the girl is working in her garden, the husband-to-be
and a friend of his suddenly swoop down upon her and carry
her off. We did not adopt the Kikuyu plan.*

*The knot being tied and the last Amen said, Miss Doering
began to play Mendelssohn's Wedding March and we
marched out as husband and wife, Grace following us. Could
not help but smile and nod at my black sisters as I passed
them.*

*Did not tarry very long outside to shake hands with the
people, for, for once, I did not care to have my pretty white
dress soiled.*

*I did shake hands with a few though.*

*How were we dressed? Well, I was in white from head to toe,
down to white slippers which I bought during my stay in
London. Must have known something of coming events! No,
really I did not.*

*Had nearly everything I needed. Also, the dress was made
here, simple and pretty. Fortunately I brought a good supply
of pretty clothes with me from home.*

*Wore two small rosebuds in my hair to please Emil and
carried a huge bouquet of roses, white, and maidenhair ferns.
The roses, picked in the garden, were like greenhouse roses at
home. Had my flowers tied with white ribbon. Wore no
ornaments except my ring and a string of pearl beads. Dear
Emil also wore a white suit, just the thing in the tropics. Never
saw him look so nice. Oh yes, he wore a rosebud too. Little*

*three-year-old Grace also in white, carried sweet peas and maidenhair ferns.*

*I arranged our flowers myself, that is, our bouquets. Also picked all the flowers for the church decorations. These, the flowers in the house, and ours, would have cost us a large sum of money at home, but here they were plentiful and the woods full of ferns.*

*We had our lunch at Mr. Hurlburt's house—Daddy's house we like to call it, for he has certainly been a father to us.*

*The house decorations were yellow and green, flowers so pretty and graceful. The dining room was beautiful. Of course, Mr. and Mrs. Sywulka sat at the head of the long table with Mr. and Mrs. Hurlburt on either side. There were sixteen grownups of us, while the children feasted in another room. Karl and Agnes Hurlburt waited on our table. What did we have for lunch? Well, it was better than I expected to have in Africa:*

*Sliced roast beef*
*Scalloped potatoes*
*Chicken salad served on lettuce leaves*
*Bread and butter*
*Olives*
*Salted almonds*
*Strawberries*
*Cream*
*Cake*

*Sent to Nairobi for the meat—about 50 miles from Kijabe. The chickens? Well, it took a man the greater part of a week to go for them and return, five days I think. The butter also came from a distance. The olives came out of my Christmas, so did the fruitcake. Mother did not know that these things would be saved for my wedding. Had two other kinds of cake besides.*

*The bride's cake was white and after the manner of weddings, I had to cut it. Am sorry I could not send you more. Ah, it did seem so nice to have something to eat from home on this day of days.*

*After lunch we spent some time in a social way. Tried to get used to being called Mrs. Sywulka instead of Miss Schneider.*

*By and by we had our pictures taken, not so very good. If possible we will send you one. Ah yes, when my dear ones at home knew about our coming wedding they ordered a dress post haste for me. At present it is somewhere between Africa and America. The last line written was, "Now for goodness' sake, Marie, don't you dare get married before that dress gets there," but the advice came about five days before we were to be married, and I would not wait for the prettiest dress ever made. Sorry to disappoint my darlings but could not help it. They really ought to have sent me a couple of strong working dresses instead for I do rip and tear my dresses so out here. Have sent home for some.*

*Somehow I hear you ask: How did Emil act before, during and after the ceremony? Every bit like a manly man. Is that saying enough?*

*After this, we changed our wedding "dub-dubs" for our "safari" traveling clothes, we would call them at home. It makes all the difference in the world if one takes the "20th Century Limited" or goes afoot in the heart of Africa. We dressed accordingly—Emil in a new khaki suit and I in short skirt and waist, also khaki and new. Ah, really we looked quite fine. Had to look after our porters to get them started with the tents, food, etc. needed for the march. Also had to look after our black boys' dog, old hen, and kettle of yeast. In the grand mix-up it is a wonder that we did not forget to get started ourselves.*

*Just before leaving we had a most blessed little benediction meeting at the Ladies' House—my old home. There was prayer and song and such kind words. A much better way of sending off bride and groom than with showers of rice and old shoes as they do at home. We had showers of blessing instead.*

*As to the wedding journey. Got started a little after 3 p.m. Five of our friends escorted us for more than an hour's walk. Took the path just back of the Ladies' House which Emil had the men make, a steady winding climb until the top of the ridge is reached.*

*One does not mind the climb very much for the path leads through such a beautiful cedar forest. Just before our friends left us, they brought out a surprise lunch basket and we had our wedding dinner over again. Just for fun our friends said that they were going with us all the way. Even had a black man lug a huge bag of bed clothes up that hill. Of course we wanted them to come with us very much?????*

*Final goodbyes were said after this lunch, they going back and we forward. We appreciated their company very much, but oh dear, it was so nice to be left alone and to each other at last. After nearly another hour's march we pitched our tent. Had to hurry for it was getting dark fast. Our twilight here lasts only about 15 minutes.*

*Some of our men helped pitch the tent while others built a nice fire. Of course we did not want much supper after a 4:30 o'clock lunch.*

*We were just on the edge of the bamboo forest which we entered the next morning. Stopped long enough to visit a village of another tribe, totally different from our people in manner and appearance. Huts built of bamboo. So after leaving them we entered a very wet place, marshy, but it was not the slough of despond that Bunyan speaks about in his Pilgrim's Progress. Whenever we got to a river or wet place my dear husband would insist on carrying me. At first I asserted my American independence, but I finally yielded and always paid toll on the other side as a bride ought to have done.*

*Much of the day we went through the bamboo forest. How shall I describe it? Well, I simply cannot, for words fail me here. The grandeur cannot be described. Tall, straight, silvery leafed. Some reaching a height of 60 feet. Thousands and thousands of trees as far as the eye could see.*

*As I looked and looked I could only compare it to some vast, silent, wonderful old cathedral. Somehow the feeling stole over me that was ours in Westminster Abbey. The bamboo reeds seemed like a thousand pipes of some huge organ, untouched, unplayed. Lest the silence be broken, nature had provided a deep carpet for our noisy feet. Somehow we felt that here dwells the Unseen Presence, Creator of all things and Lord over all.*

*Towards afternoon we again came to a clear place. About 4 p. m. we pitched our tent for the second time. All day long there had been a steady climb. We were more than 8000 feet above sea level and literally in the clouds. While the tent was being put up, I had to wrap up in a blanket, it was so wet and cold.*

*However, we soon had a nice campfire and a boiling kettle. A hot supper which we ate off the top of a box, seated on the ground, refreshed us very much. Was surprised that I stood the walk so well, for at home I simply could not walk a long distance. But then walking is much easier here on account of the high altitude. Can't say that I got so very tired at any time.*

*Next morning, stage three of our journey was begun. This was similar to the day before. Saw plenty of elephant tracks, more than a foot deep and at the least twenty-two inches across. Emil measured them with the barrel of the rifle. Part of our path the rhinoceri use. Did not see any animals for which I was most thankful. Am not very good at climbing trees. Besides, a tree does not always happen to be near when most needed. Then too, a large elephant would pull up a tree quite easily. There or then where would we have been?*

*Enjoyed the bamboo and other forests so much. As the paths are very narrow we had to walk Indian file, a long row of us, black and white. Emil, I, the dog and old hen were the only white beings. Can you imagine seeing us with all our blacks and packs?*

*Well, we were a jolly, happy company. Even the dog knew that this was no everyday safari, for he carried his head high and tail very straight.*

*After leaving the forest we had some long steep hills to climb . . . The last hill having been ascended, we came in sight of the spot we were to occupy. Could not help but sing, "I'm going home to roam no more," and here we were at home, home at last. A home such as neither of us had dreamed of while in the homeland. There is but one home after all, that established by those who have just taken upon themselves the title of husband and wife.*

*We did not have a nicely furnished house to go to. That is not necessary in order to have a home. Again we pitched our tent*

*for the third time, built an altar unto the God of our fathers
and to our God, the God who had so wonderfully united our
lives, and lo our home was established.*

*"What matters it here—a tent or a cottage," we are singing.
All glory to God. We are the children of a King. We are
extremely happy in our temporary tent house.*

*The wedding journey is ended—that first stage of our married
life. What a novel and wonderful trip it was. Not every girl has
the privilege of enjoying such a trip as I had. We walked a
distance of between thirty and thirty-five miles and through
such magnificent forests most of the way, always getting still a
little bit nearer to the vast interior of this great dark continent.*

*Every girl has a right to envy me. Really this one thing alone
was worth coming to Africa for. Perhaps because I obeyed His
voice, His "Go," all these blessings have been added unto me.
I can only say, "My cup runneth over." God is good and a
rewarder of them that diligently seek Him. My darling
husband and I feel the same; and by His grace our united lives
shall tell for God more than our single lives could possibly
tell.*

*We also consider it a most sacred privilege to establish this
new station. We are not building on another man's territory,
for no mission work has ever been done here.*

*To many, the first white woman is quite a curiosity, both as to
her appearance and her methods. Many, many people come to
greet us, always in a well-meant if not a pleasing manner. One
old, old grandmother took both my hands in her wrinkled
ones, rubbed them with a vim and at the same time poured out
copious mouthfuls of spit, rubbing it well into my hands,
grease and dirt thrown in extra. Hardly knew how to return
the compliment but did the best I knew how with smiles and
words. The grease and dirt washed off easily with the use of
plenty of soap and warm water but the good will still remains.
(4)*

Thus began a partnership which was to last for nearly forty
years despite constant changes and challenges.

They had much in common, this pioneering couple. Both were
eldest children of immigrant parents; both knew the meaning of

hard work. Both had attended Moody; both had Methodist church background. Most importantly, both had a deep love for God and for Africa.

And yet, in personality they seemed worlds apart. Emil was extremely focused and earnest; his fellow-missionaries often used the word zeal to describe him. By contrast Marie, while never idle, knew how to take herself less seriously.

Emil paid little attention to what he ate or what he wore; Marie got a good deal of pleasure out of homemaking, cooking and gardening. She liked to set a good table; by way of contrast, Emil didn't mind serving potatoes in a lid turned upside down.

There were other differences. Emil mastered language after language, while Marie struggled to communicate with the villagers through English and a limited African vocabulary. Emil's letters are full of exhortations; Marie wrote about family, friends, her menus, and the weather. Emil was forever off on evangelistic safaris, while Marie stayed home, watching and waiting. She never knew exactly when he would breeze in again, nor when he might announce, "We move tomorrow."

Almost a century later, we look back and see God's wisdom in uniting them; Marie was such a good balance for Emil. For one thing, she knew how to moderate the "tendency toward bluntness" that the old Methodist pastor had detected in him. Then, too, Emil was sometimes plagued by feelings of unworthiness. Even after years of successful ministry, he once confided that "about the only thing I ever felt I could do well was to chop wood and pull out stumps." (5) Marie's cheery, buoyant personality was a good antidote at such times.

## CONFRONTING THE WITCH DOCTOR

In the early days, when the Sywulkas lived in a tent, it was easy for petty thieves to enter their home. One day Emil found some money missing, and complained to the local chief. The chief had all the village men line up, and then asked the witch doctor to point out the thief.

The witch doctor, who undoubtedly had a good idea of the robber's identity, asked the men to hold out their hands. "The one on whom the water drops miraculously is the thief," he stated. Then he walked down the line of men, holding a gourd above their open hands. At one point, drops of water mysteriously came out of the bottom of the gourd, dripping upon the man's open hands.

"See, here is the thief!" declared the witch doctor.

Then Emil asked to hold the gourd. Holding it just as the witch doctor had done, he showed a small hole which the witch doctor had covered up until he wanted to let the drops out. The witch doctor, ashamed of being shown for what he was —a charlatan— retreated fom the area, and people began listening more readily to the Gospel.

## *IT'S A BOY!*

The Sywulkas had pitched their tent on a hilltop in a place called Matara. And yet, they returned to Kijabe from time to time. It was here that on May 28, 1908, little Paul Emil was added to their family —at the very clinic where Marie had delivered so many other babies when she was single.

**Marie and Emil with Paul**

As they tenderly cradled their first-born, Emil and Marie little dreamed what a curiosity Paul would be among people who had never before seen a white child. Nor could they have foreseen how the baby would become a magnet, drawing people to them and their message.

## *TEDDY ROOSEVELT*

The following year, the Sywulkas were back at Kijabe for another historic occasion.

Charles Hurlburt had met Teddy Roosevelt while on a recruiting trip in the USA. The president had summoned him to the White House and asked his advice about an upcoming safari.

> *Quick to recognize an opportunity, Hurlburt invited him to lay the foundation stone for Rift Valley Academy, the new school for missionaries' children at Kijabe. (6)*

**Teddy Roosevelt lays the foundation for RVA**

**AIM missionaries welcome Teddy Roosevelt**

**AIM missionaries with Teddy Roosevelt.**
**Emil, wearing pith helmet and holding Paul, stands to the left of the**
**President.**

The missionaries welcomed the president with the best they could afford. Marie prepared and served a fruitcake; the recipe came from Emil's mother, whom she had never met.

Teddy Roosevelt enjoyed the feast prepared in his honor, laid the cornerstone with plenty of pomp and ceremony, posed for photographs with the Kijabe missionaries, and then continued his safari.

### FIRST MATARA CONVERTS

Few Sywulka letters survive from the days at Matara, high on Kenya's "misty ridges," but the following story, told by an African pastor named Johana, has been recorded.

> *I was a small boy herding my father's sheep and goats. The*
> *first white man I ever saw came to our village. The women and*
> *children, very frightened, cried, "Kill a sheep and sacrifice it*
> *or we die. We looked upon a face like the face of God; it is*
> *white."*

*He was Bwana Sywulka who first opened Matara. He called*
*us together to tell us about the love of the Son of God. His*
*words were to me like the taste of honey. After a few days he*
*left our ridge to camp on another. I left my father's herd with*
*another herd boy while I went to the ridge where the tent was*
*pitched to hear more. My father gave me a beating and*
*forbade me to listen to the white man. (7)*

Time after time, Johana ran away from his hut in order to
hear more about the Son of God. When scoldings and beatings
failed to keep the youth at home, his father disinherited him.
Johana kept on listening and learning; the words he heard "burned
like a fire" in his heart and he longed to be able to read them.
Eagerly he studied the strange looking marks in Bwana Sywulka's
Book. As soon as he learned to read, he helped teach other herd
boys who also managed to escape from their duties for short
periods. And so the work grew.

When the Moody Bible Institute asked Emil for a report, he
wrote:

*Am hungry for the living God and long for the fire from*
*heaven to fall as never before and that on me. God's Word is*
*growing more real and sweeter all the time. Am learning to*
*take God at His Word in many things, that I did not before. I*
*praise Him yea and Jesus Christ whom He hath sent.*

*Since the beginning of the work here at Matara (18 months*
*ago) sixteen boys have requested to be baptized, others are*
*turning to the Lord . . . We are also experiencing strong*
*opposition for all which we praise God from our hearts. (8)*

### PERMANENT RESULTS

In time, Dr. Virginia Blakeslee joined the Sywulkas at Matara,
exercising her dual skills as physician and Bible teacher. The
concerted efforts of the three missionaries bore fruit, and the herd
boys became church leaders. Eventually, the missionaries left the
work in the hands of capable elders and pastors.

By 1909, the Sywulkas were gone from Matara, but the seed
they had planted among the Kikuyu people continued to grow, and
"new congregations multiplied across the ridges."(9)

Nearly thirty years later, Marie, while on vacation in Kenya, discovered that Johana had been called to pastor the large Kijabe church. She wrote to her son Paul:

> *Kijabe is beautiful. Great stretches of green lawns, flowers, beautiful landscaping. It is not at all like the place I knew years ago. Sunday morning I attended the native service. One of our old Matara boys is preacher there. He told the people that he knew me when I was a young woman and how he used to follow Bwana Sywulka when he was a little Shensi boy. It was through your father that he became a Christian and he has stayed true through all the years . . .*
>
> *One day your father interested the boys with a magnifying glass, concentrating the sun's rays on a sheet of paper, explaining that the power was in the sun, not in the glass, and buying up the opportunity made an illustration of it. Christ the Power, not we.*
>
> *[Johana] used that illustration that morning in his sermon. After all these years —probably 28—he had not forgotten it! Your father has certainly left an impression on many lives in many places. He just the glass —Christ the Sun and Power.*
> *(10)*

Christ, the Light behind the glass, was also the Pillar of Cloud going ahead. In 1909 the Sywulkas would see that Light beckoning them across international borders to a new country and a new people group. Great changes for them, and for the AIM, were about to take place.

**References:**

(1) Anderson, Dick, *op. cit.*, p. 38
(2) *Ibid.*, p. 54
(3) *Ibid.*
(4) Letter from Marie to Emil's parents, August 26, 1907
(5) Letter from Emil to his sisters Jeannette and Louisa, Dec. 15, 1923
(6) Anderson, *op. cit.*, p. 34
(7) *Ibid.*, p. 86
(8) Undated report from Emil to the Moody Bible Institute
(9) Anderson, *op. cit.*, p. 87
(10) Letter from Marie to her son Paul, Feb. 5, 1936

# CHAPTER 4
## German East Africa
## 1909 – 1913

### A NEW ASSIGNMENT

In her single days, Marie determined "just to do what He makes plain." In 1909, God made plain a new assignment: the Sywulkas were to move out of British East Africa, and into German East Africa (now Tanzania).

It would not be easy to leave their beloved Kikuyu and make a new start among the million-strong Sukuma people. The move would mean a new language, new customs, and a new climate—"a maelstrom of malaria."

And yet, they would not be following an uncharted path, for Anglican missionaries had already blazed the trail.

### ANGLICAN FOUNDATIONS

In 1888, the Church Mission Society opened a station at Nassa in German East Africa. In the ensuing years, they sent fifteen Anglican missionaries by turns to the area.

> Nassa in the early days was a well-wooded country, and the missionaries brought down many a zebra and impala. Those who were little boys at the time tell of how they peeped into the tent to get a glimpse of the white men (they were rare in those days), and saw one of the men smoking a curved, turned up pipe. (1)

One early Anglican missionary boarded and clothed fifty boys, teaching them in Swahili, and charging an entrance fee of millet or goats. Next came a Mr. Nickisson who used the native Sukuma tongue, taught all day until 4 p.m., then visited in the villages until after dark. The Sukuma knew that he loved them, and they never forgot him.

After only five years, Nickisson died and was buried at Nassa. Many of those who followed him also gave their lives, casualties of malaria or worse fevers, and even, in one case, a hunting accident.

The last Anglican missionaries in Nassa were the Wrights and Mr. Leach. Mrs. Wright was the first white woman missionary on the southern shores of Lake Victoria; one can imagine the curiosity she aroused.

> *Mr. Leach... was a man of prayer, getting up at 4 a.m. for*
> *fellowship at the Throne. Indefatigable in labor, he carried on*
> *the dispensary work, gave time to translation work and much*
> *else... The people said of Mr. Leach, "He is like Bwana*
> *Nickisson—gentle and kind." (2)*

Marie wrote: "These men were the trail blazers and the foundation stones upon which our AIM work is built. All honor to them!" (3)

## COME OVER TO NASSA!

The Anglican missionaries were isolated from their colleagues. Furthermore, they had little to show for their twenty years of effort. The Church Missionary Society therefore decided to give up Nassa, and to concentrate on Uganda, where results were much more promising.

In 1908, Bishop Tucker of the CMS asked Charles Hurlburt if the AIM would take over the Nassa station. Tucker and Hurlburt crossed Lake Victoria together and Hurlburt "spied out the land." After prayerful consideration, he said "Yes" to the bishop and began to ask God, "Whom shall I send?"

The answer was obvious. Emil and Marie had been in Africa only three years, but they had already distinguished themselves in pioneer leadership roles. And there was something else; they both spoke German—a big advantage in what was then German East Africa.

37

## ARRIVAL AT NASSA

The Sywulkas packed up their few belongings—Emil was adamantly opposed to amassing possessions—then crossed Lake Victoria in a German boat and disembarked in Mwanza. Like most ports, Mwanza was a crossroads of diverse nationalities: Arabs, East Indians, a few German government officials, and Africans from many tribes.

A messenger from Mr. Wright met the Sywulkas at the pier and told them how to get to Nassa. They would board another boat and head east. Marie later wrote:

> The next morning we started off for Nassa (the "we" included a year-old baby) in a little steam launch with our loads—cost, forty rupees. The journey had its adventures. Mr. Sywulka was ill all the way, and by evening had developed a hard case of double mumps!" (4)

Double mumps were not the only adventure. Soon the travelers discovered that the boat was on fire; a smoker had carelessly discarded a burning match! Fortunately, the blaze was quenched in time. Marie's account continues:

> About sundown, the whistle blew and we arrived somewhere near where the Nassa garden now is, which was the port of entrance then—date, June 29, 1909. We were heartily welcomed by the Wrights and Mr. Leach. A fine supper awaited us, but Mr. Sywulka was too sick to partake of solids, and his wife too weary. All down the long years we have remembered the soup served that evening—it touched the spot and met our physical needs. Thank you again, dear Mrs. Wright. (5)

## FIRST CHURCH SERVICE

Although Emil was still recovering from double mumps, the Sywulkas attended church on their very first Sunday at Nassa. They were eager to meet the congregation of several hundred, which they were to inherit. But the worshipers would not settle down.

*The people restlessly chattered, unsettling Mr. Wright of the
CMS until he realized that they had heard rumour of a new
baby in their midst. Borrowing Paul Sywulka from his
mother's arms, he paraded round the church so that everyone
could catch a first glimpse of a white one-year-old. Then they
quieted. (6)*

## FIRST SERMON IN SUKUMA

From the beginning, Emil applied himself vigorously to
mastering the Sukuma tongue, while Marie plunged into what she
called "dispensary work."

They also got acquainted with their new parishioners. The
Sukuma lived in round, thatched huts and engaged in subsistence
farming, mainly sweet potatoes and millet or kaffir corn. They
were entirely dependent on rainfall; if not enough fell, the crops
withered. Too much rain, on the other hand, brought severe
flooding and washed away the precious topsoil. In addition to
weather problems, there were pests. Locusts, in particular, could
wipe out an entire crop in a matter of hours.

The Sukuma lived primarily on *bugali*, a stiff corn mush
boiled over an outdoor fire. At dinnertime, each family member
took out a lump, rolled it into a ball, pressed a thumb into it, and
used the ball as a scoop for the accompanying sauce of meat,
peanuts, or greens.

By Emil's fourth Sunday in Nassa, the Anglican missionaries
were gone. He found himself facing the large congregation alone.
Amazingly, he attempted to preach in Sukuma, and the Africans
claimed to understand him!

## AN EMPTY CHURCH

It didn't take long for Emil and Marie to realize that many
Nassa parishioners "were living in sin though some could pray like
bishops." The big chapel was filled with hundreds of people every
Sunday, but they came only because the chief commanded them to
do so. Emil wrote:

> *Nothing but a God-given courage could have taken us through those days of awful disappointment and trial of faith. My preaching seemed to hit back at me. I felt no response. I told Chief Shimba and the people that I did not want people to come by compulsion. (7)*

The chief was all too glad to repeal compulsory church attendance. The next Sunday the big chapel was nearly empty! Emil announced, "Nassa will have a clean church, even if only two Christians remain."

As the weeks went by, attendance dwindled even more.

Emil felt a lump in his throat as he preached. Perhaps his challenge might come true; the church might be reduced to two members!

Emil felt that he had failed his own mission and ruined the work that the CMS had built up over twenty years. There was only one thing to do with his disappointment—take it to the Lord. Each day, he climbed the hill behind the station and devoted long hours to prayer and fasting. God heard, and Emil reported the answer to Mr. Hurlburt:

> *As far as numbers are concerned we made a tremendous failure, but I hope we have established a different conception of what it means to become, and to be, a Christian. I believe we are on the victory side. The last prayer meeting we had was the best one of all. (8)*

## A SIMPLE LIFE-STYLE

At Nassa, the Sywulkas lived in a native-style house, its floor and walls smeared with cow manure. Once dry, this smooth covering left no telltale odor. One day a visitor, running her hand over the "papered" wall asked, "Is this local or imported?"

"It's local," was the soft reply.

Like their Sukuma neighbors, the Sywulkas raised chickens and grew vegetables. Some months after settling in, they received a letter from worried colleagues in Kijabe who heard that they had "gone down, down, down in wholesome ways of living, running around bareheaded and barefooted, living on native food." Marie later recounted:

40

*This came as a complete surprise to us, and while we greatly
appreciated the dear folk being troubled about us... we were
more or less amused... We were glad to inform our friends
that we had plenty of milk from our own native cattle in the
kraal, butter, eggs, fowl, rice, fruit, and lots of fish fresh from
the lake... True, all native food! (8)*

## AN EPIDEMIC OF MENINGITIS

In 1910, Bertha Simpson was sent from Kenya to help the
Sywulkas at Nassa. Emil took off shortly, this time "into
Ntuzuland" with fellow AIM pioneer John Stauffacher. With the
goal of opening a work there, "they selected a site and buried a
bottle there containing a note, claiming that land for Jesus Christ."
(10)

After some ten days, Emil and John returned to Nassa, only to
discover that in their absence both Marie and little Paul had
contracted meningitis. This was serious indeed! And there was no
doctor or nurse anywhere in the area. Marie later wrote:

*Mr. Stauffacher had to return to Kenya at once. Then Miss
Simpson came down with the same illness, and Mr. Sywulka
had three patients to care for... Again God was our
sufficiency, and all recovered. The epidemic was a light one
and we heard of only one death in the community. (11)*

## NEW FLOORING FOR THE CHURCH

Emil and Marie had high hopes for change in the Nassa
church. They wanted to see "the reprobates and incorrigibles"
weeded out. They wanted to see less cold formality and more
genuine devotion. And they wanted to see church members serve
on a volunteer basis. Marie later reminisced:

*General changes were made slowly, including swinging over
from the Church of England service to our form of worship.
The people expected to be paid for service given to the church.
We felt that their service should be a free will offering unto the
Lord. The hard earth floor in the chapel deteriorated badly,
and the women were requested to smear the floor according to
the custom observed in their own houses and ours, with soft*

*well-mixed cow manure… Our women decided that they
would not do this work without being paid for it. So one
morning Miss Simpson and I put on our oldest duds and shoes
and got busy doing their work. After a while, one of the sisters
came by, looked in, then fled, telling the other women what we
were doing. Soon some of the women appeared and took over
the job—and without pay. (12)*

## DREADED FEVERS

While Emil was on one of his trips, Miss Simpson fell
seriously ill again—this time with malaria, a sickness that
periodically attacked both Emil and Marie. Marie wrote to Mr.
Hurlburt:

*Paul and I have been free from fever so far, a good record I
say. Wish that this could be said of my dear husband.
Sometimes I am afraid that he cannot stand this climate. I am
sure that Miss Simpson ought hardly to be here during the
rainy season. I may be mistaken. It seems good to have
another woman to talk to although I have never been
lonesome. Too busy for that. Besides, that small son of ours is
such a mischievous comfort. He refuses to talk U.S. English
but talks this language [Sukuma] and Swahili instead. Emil is
not at home at present… He will probably be gone another
week or ten days—ages to me. (13)*

Because of her health problems, it seemed best for Miss
Simpson to return to Kenya. The Sywulkas began praying that God
would send others to take her place.

## A NEW STATION: KIJIMA

In 1910, Emil, accompanied by the AIM's James Gribble,
ventured into the unreached Nera district. It was nearly three days'
hike beyond Mwanza and even farther from Nassa, but bicycles
shortened the travel time. Both men felt that Kijima, in this densely
populated area, would make an ideal mission station.

But the local people were extremely suspicious of the two
strangers. Even when Emil became desperately ill, they refused to
share their food with him. Somehow, Emil managed to make it

back to Nassa on his own, leaving James Gribble at Kijima by himself.

Emil continued to have the Nera district on his heart. He wrote to Mr. Hurlburt:

> *I think with three more workers I could take care of Nera and Nassa spending at Nassa about six months in a year, teaching and preaching, and then leaving the work in the hands of native teachers. Oh, for laborers! (14)*

## NEW WORKERS AND AN OPEN GRAVE

In early 1911, the Sywulkas sailed across Lake Victoria to Kijabe. They returned with three new workers. One of these was Dewey Van Dyke, a single man. The other two were an engaged couple: Jacob Wall and his fiancée Dora Jacobson.

As Emil and Marie crossed the lake with the new missionaries, they rejoiced that God had answered their prayers. With fresh recruits to help him, Emil could now expand into more unreached areas and also have more time for language study.

Disturbing news, however, awaited them in Mwanza. Upon disembarking, they learned that James Gribble was in the hospital! Then his story came out. Alone at Kijima, he had contracted the dreaded blackwater fever. No matter how ill he felt, he knew he must go for help. Despite burning fever and extreme weakness, he got on his bicycle, rode forty miles over the hills into Mwanza, and checked into the government hospital. There he hung between life and death, his blood count so low that his fingernails were completely white.

At Kijabe, Mr. Hurlburt had given Emil a letter for James, requesting him to return to Kenya at once. Emil and Marie wondered whether they should deliver the missive, or risk their leader's displeasure by withholding it. When they asked the doctor's advice, he answered in emphatic German, "No! He cannot go to Kenya; he will die on the way." And so, they never gave James the letter. Later they were sharply criticized for their action, but they knew they had done the right thing.

Amazingly, James Gribble later recovered enough to leave the hospital. After a time under Marie's expert nursing in Nassa, he returned to Kenya, went from there to Congo, and later laid down his life in French Equatorial Africa.

Given Gribble's condition, Emil and Marie were doubly grateful for their three new co-workers. Jacob Wall had come to Africa well aware of its perils and its numberless missionary graves. When setting out, he stated, "I feel I am to go to Africa, if only to glorify Him there by my death." (15)

His premonition came true. Three weeks after arriving at Nassa, Jacob succumbed to a tropical fever. The Sywulkas' joy over the new recruits suddenly turned to sorrow. Marie wrote:

> *We could only bow our heads and say: "I worship thee, sweet will of God, and all Thy ways adore." We buried our brother at sundown in the little cemetery below us. How our hearts went out to Miss Jacobson. The Lord gave us wonderful sustaining peace and victory. As we stood there at the grave, in spite of our tears, we sang but one song (or rather chorus) and that over and over again: Hallelujah for the Cross. (16)*

### MISS JACOBSON'S PRAYERS

Jacob Wall was dead, Dewey Van Dyke was sent to Kijima, and James Gribble returned to Kenya. Of all the new missionaries, only Dora Jacobson remained at Nassa. She had come with dreams of a wedding; when those hopes were dashed, she determined to stay on as a single person.

> *[The Sywulkas] wondered why she had come for she seemed to lack any talents. But she too knew how to pray and this became her initial ministry. She loved the solitude and the inspiration of the cemetery, hallowed by nine Anglican graves, and often spent half a day praying there. Unbelieving Sukuma thought she went there to commune with the departed. Unwise perhaps in her choice of place, God honoured her cries and hungry souls began to inquire how they might find him. The church filled again. Decades later, senior pastors and African missionaries reckoned their spiritual birth back to those prayer vigils. (17)*

44

## THE CHAPEL FILLS UP AGAIN

Revival sparks were kindled earlier when Emil spent "long hours of prayer and fasting" on the hill behind the station. But now the flames blazed brightly. The chapel filled up once again, and people even came to Emil asking how to be saved. Christians began asking how they could share the Good News.

One day two men came pleading, "Please let us go and take the words of God to others who know Him not. May we go?"

Emil replied, "With all my heart I want you to go, but have no money with which to send you."

"Money! We want no money, only let us go," the men insisted. And so they went. What an encouragement for Miss Jacobson and the Sywulkas.

## A NEW BABY AND A PROLONGED ILLNESS

On June 20, 1911, little Edward Frederick Sywulka came into the world prematurely. Marie was ill at the time, but only Miss Jacobson and a Greek woman were on hand to deliver the baby and nurse the mother.

Six months later, Marie was stricken with a long siege of typhoid. She was forced to spend three months in bed, with no one to look after her except Miss Jacobson. Dora knew nothing about professional nursing, but she had the gift of "helps" as well as that of prayer, and she was able to make Marie comfortable.

It must have been hard for Marie to lie in bed and not be able to care for three-year-old Paul and baby Edward. She wrote:

> *Yes, we were near death's door and the days were hard days*
> *for all concerned, but praise God, "The healing of the*
> *seamless dress is by our beds of pain, We touch Him in life's*
> *throng and press, And we are whole again." (18)*

**Baby Edward with Marie and Paul**

**The Sywulka boys ride in a goat cart**

Few Sywulka letters survive from the Nassa days, but Emil's family preserved his 1911 Christmas letter to them:

*Dear Ones in the Home Land,*

*I ought not to have said "Homeland" for I for one have felt that is truly my homeland. Where Jesus is, is home to me.*

*How are you our loved ones? Thank you for your letter, [brother] Edward, and for yours, Louisa. Also very many thanks for the $30 of which we have not yet heard but hope to soon.*

*Our Father supplies all our needs. We are all well at present. Paul had sore eyes but is better. Edward is growing fine. I have been away for almost a month during October to Nera where we have a new mission station. It's about 90 miles from here. There are 70,000 people in Nera.*

*I'm afraid this must be your Christmas letter. It may reach you in time by the barest possibility. Behold I bring you good tidings of great joy to all the people for unto you is born this day in the city of David a Savior which is Christ the Lord.*

47

*What can I wish you but the experience of the inborn indwelling Christ as your Christmas joy. Just think that if Christ had not come we might be in the same condition as these poor people about here who are "dead in trespasses and sins." "Without hope and without God in the world," "enmity against God," "like sheep gone astray," "from the sole of the foot even unto the head there is no soundness in it, but wounds and bruises and putrefying sores; they have not been closed neither bound up, neither mollified with oil." Such is God's description of the human heart whether covered by a black body or a white. If we consider the coming of Christ in the light of this, then Christmas will take on new meaning.*

*Again I wish for you to know Jesus, for to know him is life and he who has him not is in everlasting death. This letter is for all of you and is sent together with love and prayers, Yours affectionately, Emil (19)*

## SIX WEEKS AT NERA

Due to illness, Mr. Van Dyke—like Mr. Gribble before him—was forced to leave Kijima. To make sure the work there wouldn't die, Emil headed for the Nera district, leaving his little family and Miss Jacobson alone at Nassa. On the way home, he wrote to his sister Hattie:

*We are few here and the field of service large, and unless the Lord Jehovah helped us, we would have to give up in despair for the very magnitude of it.*

*I have been away from home about six weeks now... One of our missionaries, Mr. Van Dyke, had to leave... on account of fever and so I went to Nera to look after things. Mr. Van Dyke is hardly expected back as he has had fever four times... I rather think that when I get to Nassa, Marie and I and the children will pack up and go to Nera, leaving Miss Jacobson and the native teachers to take care of the work at Nassa.*

*I am well and happy. Have had no fever for a long time and in the service of the Lord here I find plenty both of sorrow and of joy and we need rain and sunshine to mellow our lives and make them fruitful through the Holy Spirit. (See Gal. 5:22). However, there is no service that we can possibly do, that is*

48

*more potent for the bringing of humanity to God, than the*
*service of prayer. It is not limited by distance, education,*
*poverty, [or] men's prejudice... It is only limited by two*
*things, viz. unbelief and our not giving time to prayer, or*
*both... Have you yet entered this life of prayer? You only*
*learn to pray by praying. Give God first place in your life.*
*(20)*

## FIVE NEW MISSIONARIES

As things turned out, the Sywulkas did not have to pack up
and move to Nera.

In 1913, Emil attended a field council meeting at Kijabe and
presented the crying need for new workers. When he returned, five
new recruits accompanied him: Rev. William Maynard and his
wife Dr. Nina Maynard, Miss Gertrude Bowyer, Mr. Willard
Green, and Mr. Rudolph Malek. No one bothered to let Marie
know that they were coming. She recalled:

> *On the afternoon of their arrival at Nassa, we and our African*
> *helper were about the King's business in the dispensary,*
> *cleaning house, and we looked it. Seeing a shadow on the*
> *wall, we turned around... and there stood two ladies who*
> *introduced themselves as Dr. Maynard and Miss Bowyer, and*
> *also informed us that the rest of the party would be along*
> *soon. Our prayer for more laborers was answered." (21)*

With the unexpected joy came the need for providing "sudden,
unlooked-for and unplanned-for hospitality" for the new arrivals. It
was not the first such emergency Marie would face, nor was it the
last. She continues:

> *Naturally our thoughts flew kitchen and pantryward. Being*
> *alone with two little folks meant that while we had enough*
> *good food, the shelves were not loaded down with a lot of*
> *extras... As always, the Lord met the need. It was a rare thing*
> *to have a man come with fish late in the afternoon, but that*
> *day, there he was! About the same time a man appeared with*
> *the hindquarter of a buck... There were vegetables from the*
> *garden, too. All this made a lasting impression on Dr.*
> *Maynard and Miss Bowyer. A few hours after their arrival*
> *they, as new missionaries, had their first lesson taught them...*
> *"He prepareth a table before me." (22)*

## ANOTHER BIRTH AND ANOTHER DEATH

Still another new missionary, Frank Millen, was assigned to take Dewey Van Dyke's place at Kijima. But the fever that pushed both James Gribble and Dewey Van Dyke out of Nera was about to find another victim.

In May 1913, the Sywulkas heard that Frank was ill, so they sent Rudolph Malek to see him. Rudolph mounted a bicycle and set out. Marie writes:

> *The bicycle broke down at Magu and Mr. Malek had to walk the rest of the way. He left Nassa on Monday and reached Kijima on Friday at 9:00 a.m. When he arrived at the door, he heard a native boy... weeping inside. Mr. Malek went in and found that our brother had departed to be with the Lord that very morning, May 7, 1913 (we think blackwater fever)... And so we have a missionary's grave at Kijima. (23)*

Back in Nassa, the other missionaries had no inkling of their co-worker's death. They were all rejoicing in the birth of a new baby! Little Anna Elizabeth Sywulka, named for both her grandmothers but always called "Betty," made her appearance on May 8.

This time there was a real doctor on hand for the delivery—Nina Maynard. The other women missionaries—Miss Bowyer, Miss Jacobson, and Miss Steckel—also gathered around Marie to celebrate the happy occasion. They brought goodies and spread a feast out on the bed. Someone remarked, "Why, it's just like Christmas!"

At that moment, Emil walked into the room and walked out again without saying a word. Marie recalls:

> *We though it a bit strange. After a little he came back again and brokenly told us the sad news. In a moment our rejoicing was turned into deep sorrow and weeping. What a shock! Again the loving God of all comfort met our need. (24)*

Those who remained carried on. Only a few weeks later, Nassa's missionary men were out on the road again. Marie wrote to the AIM home office:

*Just a few hasty lines from Nassa. Mr. Sywulka, Mr. Maynard,
and Mr. Melek are leaving on a safari today to be gone about
three weeks... I hate to have Mr. Sywulka go as he is far from
strong due to a recent illness...*

*Just at present we are all well except little Edward who is also
down with malaria... I trust we will have mosquito-proof
houses some of these days... Little Elizabeth now a month old
is doing splendidly and is such a joy. (25)*

## A THIRD STATION—KOLA NDOTO

Emil traveled widely, sometimes on foot and sometimes by
bicycle, usually sleeping in African homes and eating *bugali* with
his hosts around their fire. Wherever he went, he was on the
lookout for new mission sites. So he was glad when the new
missionaries opened a station at Kola Ndoto (Busia).

In September 1913, the Maynards, Gertrude Bowyer, and
Dora Jacobson left for Kola Ndoto to establish the third AIM
station in German East Africa. It was a ten-day journey, on foot all
the way. Each night they set up their tents, and each morning they
folded them up. When they reached Kola Ndoto, they lived in
those same tents until better shelters could be erected.

Mr. Maynard was a gifted leader; his wife was a skilled
physician. God blessed their efforts, and despite extremely difficult
beginnings, the Busia station eventually became one of AIM's
largest.

## FURLOUGH PLANS

The Sywulkas accomplished much in their four years in
German East Africa. Not only did they build up the Nassa work;
they helped open two additional stations and witnessed the
spiritual birth of many Sukuma people.

Emil also revised the 1896 Sukuma Gospel of John, originally
translated by Anglican missionaries. Without any of the modern
aids or linguistic courses available to contemporary translators, he
finished the revision and printed it himself on a small hand press in
1913.

Emil and Marie felt they could leave the work in other hands for a few months. In September 1913, they reached Kenya, en route to what they foresaw as a short trip to the USA. Emil had his heart set on being back in Nassa by August 1914.

They had left Nassa on faith, without funds for the passage to America. Emil even suggested that if there wasn't enough money for the whole family to travel, he and little Paul could go on ahead. On October 22, Marie wrote to AIM headquarters:

> *We found it very hard to leave our dear people and the work and I am even now counting the time when we shall again return... It is possible that Mr. Sywulka and Paul go on first, as Mr. Sywulka wants to return by next August to attend a conference in German East Africa. I can hardly bear the thought of such a plan as we need each other's help on the voyage... I have had to boost up my courage and faith... by praying often and singing too... I praise God that I know He will supply.*
>
> *The Sunday before we left Nassa, thirteen more of our people were baptized. May one and all be kept by the power of God. (26)*

Five days later, the passage money was in hand. This time it was Emil who sent off a note to the home office:

> *We have been here at Kijabe for more than a month and now God has very graciously and in an unexpected way supplied the means for our going to America. We now expect, God willing, to leave Mombasa Nov. 3. (27)*

As Emil and Marie boarded the ship, they could not have imagined how long their furlough would last, nor how much their fellow-workers would suffer in their absence. For the Great War was about to engulf the world and its effects would be felt in every continent.

**References:**

(1)  Sywulka, Marie, *Workers together with Him*, p. 3
(2)  *Ibid.*, p. 4
(3)  *Ibid*, p. 6

(4)  *Ibid*, p. 7
(5)  *Ibid*.
(6)  Anderson, *op cit.*, p 54
(7)  Sywulka, Marie, *Workers together with Him*, p. 8
(8)  Letter from Emil to Charles Hurlburt, Nov. 17, 1910
(9)  Sywulka, Marie, *Workers together with Him*, p. 10
(10) *Ibid*, p. 11
(11) *Ibid*.
(12) *Ibid*.
(13) Letter from Marie to Charles Hurlburt, Sept. 8, 1910
(14) Letter from Emil to Charles Hurlburt, Nov. 17, 1910
(15) Anderson, *op cit.*, p 55
(16) Sywulka, Marie, *Workers together with Him*, p. 16-17
(17) Anderson, *op. cit.*, p 55
(18) Sywulka, Marie, *Workers together with Him*, p. 15
(19) Letter from Emil to his siblings, Oct. 11, 1911
(20) (20)Letter from Emil to his sister Hattie, July 12, 1912
(21) Sywulka, Marie, *Workers together with Him*, p. 16
(22) *Ibid.*, p. 17
(23) *Ibid*.
(24) *Ibid*.
(25) Letter from Marie to the AIM, June 17, 1913
(26) Letter from Marie to the AIM, Oct. 22, 1913
(27) Letter from Emil to the AIM, Oct. 27, 1913

# CHAPTER 5
# The Great War
# 1914 – 1917

## *ARRIVAL IN THE USA*

The *Cincinnati* docked in New York in late December 1913. Friends from the AIM home office in Brooklyn welcomed Emil and Marie warmly, then saw them off to Ohio, where they'd celebrate a belated Christmas with Marie's family and visit her home church.

**First furlough - Edward, Paul, Betty, Marie, Emil**

Marie's mother was thrilled to meet Emil and the three new grandchildren for the first time. Young Paul and Edward, too, were excited. It was their first experience with sleds and snow.

Emil and Marie didn't expect to have a long furlough. In fact, Emil wanted to stay only six months. They could not have imagined that their furlough would stretch out, not to six months, but to more than seven years.

Emil felt unwell; he had lost weight. Yet he immediately began making plans for a trip west. He wrote to headquarters:

> *I do not feel well yet but expect, if I am able, to go to Chicago... for ten days. From there... to California via the Santa Fe Railroad...*

> *The Sunday School of the Calvary Evangelical Church, to which my wife still belongs, gave us a reception... with $40.15. (1)*

## "IN THE ABSCESS BUSINESS"

Marie, too, was unwell. She wrote to her friend Martha Young at the AIM Home Office with news of her health and Emil's travels:

> *Since before Christmas I have not been at well. Have been having a series of abscesses of the breast... the constant pain and loss of sleep finally put me to bed where I spent two weeks... I miss Mr. Sywulka very much. He expects to be at Meadows tomorrow among the Mennonite Brethren... As soon as I am well enough I hope to visit some of the churches. I do need your prayers that the message will have power. The little people are quite well. Paul is in kindergarten. (2)*

Three weeks later, she sent off an update:

> *You will be glad to know that for the past week I have been able to go out some each day although I am still in the abscess business. Mr. Sywulka had hoped to be with his parents last Saturday. (3)*

## THE GOLDEN STATE

By February of 1914, Emil had worked his way all across the nation and was with his parents. In 1910, they had moved from Wisconsin to California. There they bought a ranch in Visalia, in the fertile San Joaquin valley, and raised peaches and walnuts.

It was Emil's first glimpse of the Golden State. He marveled at the lush landscape, green even in winter, and at the snow-capped Sierra Nevada in the distance. But his thoughts were still very much in Africa. So many unevangelized villages! So few workers! He wondered why Mr. Hurlburt kept new missionaries at Kijabe instead of fanning them out to the unreached areas. From his parents' home, he wrote to the AIM:

> *I arrived here at my home safely and happily and am enjoying my stay here much. The spiritual burden of my folks are as a burden but I have committed it to Him. The world seems so needy everywhere.*

> *In about a month or so I expect to return to Los Angeles for a week or more as there are many open doors and then come back here for another short stay before going East...*

> *I have felt constrained for several months to point out to our dear brother Hurlburt the wrong of keeping so many workers at Kijabe, but I have not done it yet for I do not want to fall into Satan's snare. It does, however, grieve me intensely to think of the great needy dying world... and that so many workers should be kept at Kijabe to minister to a small number of people who have heard the Gospel a thousand times and more. (4)*

## "DOING SOME DEPUTATION"

While Emil was thousands of miles away in California, Marie's health was improving, but very, very slowly. Antibiotics were unknown, and the only remedies for abscesses were frequent lancings and heat lamp treatments. The bitter Ohio winter turned to spring; and still she was still not completely well. She wrote to Martha Young, not only confiding about her physical problems, but also expressing dismay over Emil's wish to return to Africa so soon:

> *I am still not well. Had another incision made two weeks*
> *ago... I do trust that there is not another abscess forming. The*
> *Lord has a purpose in all this and I will trust His love.*
>
> *Emil still expects to go back in June or July. I wish that he*
> *would get over that notion. He has not gained as he ought to*
> *have done. I hardly feel like returning so soon... neither do I*
> *want him to go to that malaria country alone. (5)*

The days continued to grow longer, the Akron trees leafed out and flowers bloomed in every front yard. By May, Marie was taking speaking engagements even though the abscess was not completely healed. She wrote from Cleveland:

> *Emil is still not at home... I am in the "Forest City" at Miss*
> *Bowyer's old home. Previous to this I spent about ten days*
> *with other friends in this city doing some deputation work. . .*
>
> *I am here taking treatment, for my breast is not well yet, but*
> *getting much better now. The intense heat and light of a 500*
> *candle power electric light and vibrations are doing me much*
> *good and I believe that we will not have to use the knife... I*
> *have had a hard and long siege, going on five months, but I*
> *am of good courage and praise God for all His goodness...*
>
> *Our little people are doing nicely. I left them in Akron and*
> *miss them oh so much. Hope to see them Friday. Emil may be*
> *home by that time. He has not been so well of late. (6)*

## *"I HAVE NO STEREOPTICON"*

When Emil returned to Akron, he could see at a glance that Marie was in no condition to return to Africa. But he still hoped to sail in June—by himself—so that he could attend the August Kilimanjaro conference. In late May, he wrote to the home office:

> *I trust and pray that I may be able to return to Africa about*
> *the latter part of June. I do not think that my wife will be ready*
> *to return at that time. (7)*

By June, reality set in. Emil *wouldn't* be going back to Africa immediately. He *wouldn't* make the Kilimanjaro conference. Leaving his disappointment with God, he busied himself with "Plan B"—contacting still more churches in hopes of presenting Africa's need. He must have found that some groups were looking for speakers with attractive visual aids—stereopticons or "magic lanterns" which could project images on a screen. He had none. So he wrote to headquarters:

> *If you know of churches that would like to hear about the Gospel's power and the need of it in Africa, let me know. Who will wake up the churches of America to their responsibility and restore their lost vision? My soul is exceedingly burdened and grieved over the awful apathy, indifference and selfishness of our boasted Christianity... Now I have no stereopticon but I believe I have a message from God should there be opportunity to present it.*
>
> *Thus far it does not seem as though I'll get to the Kilimanjaro Conference as I had planned, but God's way is best, whichever way it will be. (8)*

## WAR!

Within weeks, terrifying news hit the headlines. The tinderbox which was Europe had exploded; its nations were at war. Eventually Austria, Germany, and the other Central Powers would be aligned against Russia, Great Britain, and their allies.

The effects of the war would be truly global, and one of the arenas of fighting would be German East Africa. Realizing that the war might temporarily close the door to his field, Emil committed yet another disappointment to the Lord and wrote to headquarters:

> *Should the way to Africa close for the present and we be compelled to stay here through the coming winter, we'd like to go to California where my folks are. It is blessed to know that we can leave it all to Him. Had good meetings in Port Huron. (9)*

By mid-October, after holding meetings in various Ohio and Indiana cities, Emil boarded a train for California. This time, Marie and the children were with him. It was a long trip, punctuated by stops to visit churches in Chicago, Kansas, and Denver.

Every time Emil and Marie opened a newspaper along the way, there was more war news. As early as November 1914, a quarter of a million British and Indian troops invaded German East Africa. A much smaller force of Germans and Africans, under General von Lettow-Vorbeck, managed to hold them at bay.

When they left for furlough, the Sywulkas expected the new missionaries to carry on the work. But now most of those recruits, too, had left the field. Some were on furlough; others were reassigned to Kenya. One of them, Willard Green, was taken by the Germans as a prisoner of war.

During the war years, the AIM team in German East Africa was reduced to a mere three missionaries on only one station: the Maynards and Miss Bowyer at Kola Ndoto. It was only later that Emil and Marie learned how terribly their fellow workers had suffered. For twenty-six months, there was no mail service. No checks from America! William Maynard killed game, then traded the meat to local Africans for native cornmeal and rice. His wife, Dr. Nina Maynard, was struck three times with the dreaded blackwater fever. Amazingly, she survived.

## RANCH LIFE IN CALIFORNIA

While war raged in Europe and Africa, the Sywulkas watched a new spring appear in California. Marie wrote:

> *Paul has just come home with an armful of pussy willows. Every day I hear the music of the meadowlark. Oh, we see plenty of snow too, for to the east of us lie the Sierra Nevada mountains, snow capped and beautiful. Last winter was pretty hard on me after the tropics. The climate here is much better for us, and we ought to be in good condition for Africa when God sees best to send us out again. . .*

> *We do get so homesick for Africa... Emil is worse than I am. He has been busy pruning peach and walnut trees. Has finished about 500 with nearly 300 more to do. This on his people's small ranch. We are learning many things here which will be a help to us and the people, I trust, in Africa. (10)*

The peach grove became a sacred place for Emil. Here he promised God that he'd devote at least three hours a day to prayer. He prayed for God to work in his own heart, he interceded for his family and his Nassa converts, and he prayed that God would send him back to Africa.

**Betty, Edward and Paul on horseback in Visalia**

Emil couldn't go back to German East Africa, because war was still raging there. And he might also be barred from British East Africa, because he was still officially "an Austrian." As such, the British would consider him an enemy. If only he could become a naturalized American citizen! He wrote to the AIM:

> *We hadn't heard any "mission news" for a long time and only very recently had intimations that a party of missionaries had sailed. So we were glad to hear the fact of our missionaries being able to return. It makes us hungry to be sailing too. We only came out to California because we thought that it would not be possible to return, and also my wife feared to go through another winter in the East after the experience of last winter. If we could be of service in British East Africa, pending the re-opening of German East Africa, we should like, D.V., to be preparing for our return...*

> *Could you find out if I would be hindered in missionary labors
> in British East Africa seeing I am an Austrian. I tried to
> attain... U.S. citizenship on the fact that I lived here for 24
> years previous to going to Africa, but was not accepted. (11)*

Meanwhile, Marie reported on the ministry opportunities she
and Emil found in California:

> *Emil was at Farmersville last night where he conducts a Bible
> study every Wednesday evening. Sunday next he has another
> appointment elsewhere. I have a little Sunday School every
> Sunday p.m. in a nearby country school house. Emil also has a
> Monday evening Bible study in the neighborhood. So I trust
> that we are doing a little good. People here are not hungry.
> We find hearts waiting for the Bread of Life in Africa.
> Continue to pray that we may go back...*
>
> *The weather is fine here and things are growing fine. Every
> day I go out to a little stream in the "back lot" and pick a
> gunnysack of grass for the chickens. Can you picture me
> bringing it home on my back? (12)*

The Sywulkas spent the better part of 1915 in California.
Always they were waiting: waiting for news from Africa, waiting
for the war to end, waiting for permission to return to their beloved
field. By August, they felt they had lived long enough with Emil's
family. It was time to head back east, look for a little place they
could call their own, and get Paul settled in school. Emil wrote:

> *Mrs. Sywulka expects to leave here August 21 for Los Angeles
> and after a stay of ten days there to go on direct to Akron
> arriving there Sept. 4... I also expect to leave soon for the East
> but intend to spend three or four months on the way telling of
> Africa's need wherever God will open doors. D. V., will stop
> at San Francisco, Lodi California, Denver, and in Nebraska,
> etc. (13)*

### *THREE UPSTAIRS ROOMS*

Back in Akron, Marie found three second-story rooms to rent.
She wrote in early 1916:

*God only knows how much we suffer in being here. He knows
too that we would still be there. Africa is the dearest place in
all the world to us.*

*I trust that our being compelled to stay here does not mean an
entire loss, and that we are doing some good here. Husband is
in Nebraska... I miss him very much though we are in a little
corner of our own and it does seem so good. Only three rooms
but it is home. Upstairs rooms but quite comfortable. I enjoy
the housekeeping... Just at present I am busy sewing. Have
rented a machine for a month. I am praying for a machine of
my own...*

*The little folks tie me down pretty much so I do not get about
as much as I would like to do deputation work... Yes, these are
testings of faith but He has never failed us. I do praise Him.
(14)*

## "HOLINESS" CONTACTS

Emil was always happy to speak in any kind of church, to
believers of any theological stripe. In Iowa, he found "Holiness"
Christians who were eager to hear his message.

Emil felt attracted to the "Holiness" emphasis on revival, and
the movement's Wesleyan roots struck a common chord with him.

The "Holiness Movement" came about at the end of the
nineteenth century, when some earnest believers came to feel that
Methodism had lost its initial emphasis on holy living, "perfect
love," and "Christian perfection." They longed for a fresh
outpouring of the Holy Spirit.

The resulting "Holiness Movement" sought to renew John
Wesley's emphasis on sanctification as a "second work of grace"
following conversion. Holiness preachers called the believer to a
life of spiritual purity and perfection. By the turn of the century,
over 25 "Holiness" groups had sprung up in the United States. One
of these, The Pentecostal Holiness Church, was founded in 1898
and continues to this day.

Emil was even invited to speak at the Central Holiness
University in University Park, Iowa. Founded in 1906 as a

coeducational institution, it was also the site of the annual camp meeting of the National and Iowa Holiness Associations.

Emil was aware that back at AIM headquarters, there had been some question as to whether candidates with "Holiness" views should be accepted. But Emil felt strongly that Africa needed missionaries, even "Holiness" missionaries. Why should the AIM turn down those whom God had called? In a letter written in early 1916, he expressed himself frankly to the Home Office:

> *The Lord opened a number of doors to me among holiness*
> *people in Iowa though I did not seek to enter and manifestly*
> *blessed my messages to them. A number heard the call of*
> *heathenism. Was invited to come back and speak at their big*
> *Camp Meeting in June... May we not grieve His Holy Spirit*
> *nor hinder His plan. (15)*

### DREAMS OF TRANSLATION

When he returned to Akron, Emil kept thinking and praying about what he could do for the Sukuma people. Perhaps, if he couldn't go to Africa, he could bring an African to America, and together they could work on Bible translation. He wrote to Mr. Hurlburt at Kijabe:

> *How we wish we were there. We can hardly stand it. If we*
> *knew that the war will last much longer we'd have the German*
> *East Africa folks bring a native along when they come to*
> *America and I'd give my time to translating the Bible. Pray*
> *about this. (16)*

God's Word was powerful! If the Sukuma people had more of it in their language, it could do wonders for them, whether missionaries were present or not. And it could reach immigrants in Akron, too, whether or not Emil could speak their language. He wrote to a pastor friend:

> *I've often thought of you since we met in Chicago about three*
> *years ago. How are you? I am giving some of my time to*
> *colportage work (Bible portions) among the many foreigners*
> *in this city. What the Lord has for me this summer I do not*
> *know. Was in the West last summer. . .*

*We're longing to be back in dark Africa. We want our
imprisonment here to work out for His glory too. Wish I had a
native here for translation work. (17)*

Emil's idea turned out to be just one more unfulfilled dream.
He himself couldn't get the proper papers to leave America! How
could he expect someone from a German colony to gain entrance
to America? For by the spring of 1917, the United States had
declared war on Germany. Once again, Emil expressed his longing
to become an American citizen. He wrote to the AIM's Howard
Dinwiddie:

*The fact of our brother Stauffacher's at last being permitted to
go through British territory raised a hope in our hearts that
possibly a similar favor might be granted us. Somehow I have
an assurance that I believe comes from God that He is
undertaking for us.*

*And thus I wish that you would, if thus led, submit our case to
the proper authorities. We have waited so long and the need is
so urgent. . .*

*It will be two years in March since I took out my first
American citizenship papers. As you no doubt know, I am an
Austrian by birth. My parents came to America when I was
three years and six months old.*

*On account of the young man's marriage where we are
staying, we find it necessary to move in a few weeks. We do
not know yet where but God has a place for us. (18)*

The routine had by now become familiar to Marie: pack and
move; pack and move again. Of course God had a place for them!
What they couldn't have foreseen is that God had *several* more
places for them. There would be other moves before they would
see Africa again.

### References

(1) Letter from Emil to the AIM, Jan. 5, 1914
(2) Letter from Marie to Martha Young, Jan. 24, 1914
(3) Letter from Marie to Martha Young, Feb. 17, 1914
(4) Letter from Emil to the AIM, Feb. 11, 1914

(5)  Letter from Marie to Martha Young, March 19, 1914
(6)  Letter from Marie to Martha Young , May 4, 1914
(7)  Letter from Emil to Martha Young, May 20, 1914
(8)  Letter from Emil to the AIM, June 12, 1914
(9)  Letter from Emil to the AIM, Aug. 17, 1914
(10) Letter from Emil to Martha Young, Jan. 29, 1915
(11) Letter from Emil to the AIM, Feb. 3, 1915
(12) Letter from Marie to Martha Young, March 18, 1915
(13) Letter from Emil to Martha Young, August 12, 1915
(14) Letter from Marie to Martha Young, Jan. 13, 1916
(15) Letter from Emil to Mr. Palmer of the AIM, Feb. 28, 1916
(16) Letter from Emil to Charles Hurlburt, March 5, 1917
(17) Letter from Emil to Rev. J. Hagne, May 25, 1917
(18) Letter from Emil to Howard Dinwiddie, Nov. 14, 1917

# CHAPTER 6
## Bandages and Shoes for Africa
## 1918

### *AKRON, OHIO*

The Sywulkas made Akron their 1918 headquarters. Marie was glad to be near her family and her church; she did her best to make her temporary quarters a haven for Emil between his speaking engagements. The family lived for a time in a farm house where Marie's widowed mother worked as a cook for the landlord. Then they moved into town, where a novel sight—electric lights—dazzled the children.

Paul and Edward attended a one-room school. At lunchtime, they gathered at an old pump, where the all the children drank from a common pail and a single dipper.

### *A. W. TOZER*

The family attended Marie's German-speaking home church: Calvary Evangelical. But through his speaking engagements, Emil came in contact with the Christian and Missionary Alliance and met one of its greatest thinkers and pastors: Dr. A. W. Tozer. Marie's nephew John Snyder recalled those days:

> *During World War I Uncle Emil and Aunt Marie were not able to return to Africa so they lived in Akron... At that time our family was attending the German Methodist Church... All I can remember is long sermons in German which I couldn't understand...*

> *While Uncle Emil was in Akron he taught a Bible class for Chinese people at the Locust Street Christian and Missionary Alliance Church. It was through his influence that we started*

*to attend there. The old German church was declining
spiritually at that time and the new teaching on the
"Victorious Life" or the "Deeper Life" that we heard in the
Christian and Missionary Alliance was received by my parents
with great joy. (1)*

Emil and Dr. Tozer became intimate friends; they spent many
hours together on their knees. Later Tozer would write:

*One of the saintliest men I have ever known was Rev. Emil
Sywulka, a missionary of the Africa Inland Mission. His whole
life was literally a poured-out libation to His Saviour.
Suffering, sacrifice, toil and prayer were his daily
companions. (2)*

*We prayed together many long hours for the work of God. We
would agree to meet to pray. When I got there Emil would be
on his knees, weeping with tears, naming names I had never
heard, of black boys over there in Africa, begging God to have
mercy on them and to keep them strong and bless them. (3)*

## *BANDAGES FOR AFRICA*

While Emil was traveling about the country or teaching Bible
classes to Chinese immigrants, Marie was speaking to church
women's groups, challenging them to collect clothing and roll
bandages for Africa. That was something she could do for her
beloved field, even while so far away. The following letter is just
one of many she wrote to headquarters on this subject:

*Dear Brother Fletcher: We have a lot of bandages....some
bags for the natives, and clothing for our children at Dr.
Maynard's station.*

*We are wondering if these things could go as excess baggage
with the September party?*

*The things mentioned will meet a real need out there,
especially the bandages, and ought to be on the way soon. We
would meet all expenses. (4)*

Some of the parcels Marie prepared arrived in Africa; others
did not. Once, when she mailed three packages, all three were

returned to her by the New York Post office with a note stating that there was still no mail delivery at Mwanza.

But she persisted. When there was no missionary to take the bandages by boat, Marie tried the mail again.

At least one package reached Dr. Nina Maynard. Marie earmarked the bandages for the Kola Ndoto dispensary; she could not have known that Dr. Maynard would have desperate need of them to treat her own husband, Rev. William Maynard. Marie later reported:

> *The parcel was a long time reaching the coast... and if we remember rightly, was held up at the coast for six months, all due to war conditions. Finally it reached Dr. Maynard. A few days later, Mr. Maynard was badly mauled by a leopard, and the surgical dressings met the need. Dr. Maynard wrote: "If those dressings had reached here sooner, there would not have been a shred left to meet the present need." God's appointed time! (5)*

### SHOES FOR MISS BOWYER

The missionaries on the field experienced other miraculous provisions. Gertrude Bowyer's shoes wore out. With great reluctance, she informed Mr. Maynard that she could no longer engage in village visitation. Where in all of war-torn German East Africa could she find new shoes? And even if she found some, how could she pay for them when checks from America were not getting through?

It was then that Nina Maynard pulled out a pair of new shoes. "Marie Sywulka ordered these back in 1913," Nina explained. "They didn't come before her furlough, so she asked me to hold on to them when they arrived. She told me to pass them along to someone who could wear them. Take them; they're yours!"

When Marie heard the story, she thought of the verse, "Before they call I will answer." And she started collecting shoes for outgoing missionaries, along with clothing for African children and bandages for the dispensary. She mailed more packages to headquarters and wrote:

*The package marked* shoes *may be opened and if any of the ladies can wear them, they are more than welcome to them... They were given by a dear friend of the Mission very cleanly and refined. Africa makes large demands on shoe leather. (6)*

## LETTERS FROM AFRICA

Despite the postal problems occasioned by the war, some mail from Africa did get through to the Sywulkas. It was with great joy that Emil opened letters from two of his African parishioners who were growing in faith. What could thrill his heart more than to hear that his spiritual children were walking with the Lord?

It was late October, and Emil was in Indiana. He had hoped for speaking engagements, but churches were not scheduling meetings. The 1918 flu epidemic had shut their doors.

With extra time on his hands, Emil sat down, translated the letters into English and sent them off to headquarters, with this explanation about the writers:

*John Nyanda is a hunchback of German East Africa whom I visited in his village one morning about seven years ago. I believe he was born into God's family that morning. Soon his father moved away to another district. When I visited my hunchback friend some six months later I found that he had been gathering the people every night by the light of a fire of sticks and teaching them the gospel and to my unspeakable joy I found a little company that loved my Lord Jesus. It is his letter I am sending you.*

*Simeon Shigela is a young man whom I taught printing in German East Africa and who now labors at Kijabe. (7)*

## PEACE AT LAST

On November 11, 1918, the Armistice was signed. The Sywulkas watched as Akron celebrated the end to the long conflict. Some people tied boiler tubs to their cars, then drove them up and down the streets, clanking and honking all the way.

Half a world away, the troops in German East Africa kept on fighting. General von Lettow-Vorbeck refused to surrender until three days after the signing of the Armistice in Europe.

Only then was the Great War truly over. It had caused untold deprivation and suffering in German East Africa. Even the missionaries had not been spared. Willard Green, a Canadian, remained a prisoner of war until the British took over. He was then released, but two German missionaries were subsequently interned by the British!

The war also directly impacted Marie's own family. Her sister Lizzie's husband had to leave Akron to fight for the Allies. In the opposing army, a Wiegand cousin fought for the Kaiser and fell in 1917 in Rumania, leaving two small sons to be raised by their mother. In a masterful understatement, Marie wrote: "War is war."

But now it was all over, and the Sywulkas once more allowed themselves to think about returning to Africa. Just days after the Armistice was signed, Marie wrote to headquarters:

> I am going to begin to get ready for our return although I haven't a thing to go on but the "exceeding great and precious promises to usward" and God is able to bring them all to pass in His own time and way. (8)

Great changes, however, were in store for Tanganyika. After months of deliberation, the League of Nations decided to mandate the entire territory—five million people comprising more than 100 tribes—to Great Britain. Suddenly, what had been *German* East Africa became *British* East Africa. Rupees were replaced by shillings; businesses and government offices were forced to switch from German to English. In all this, no one bothered to consult the African people themselves. They were but pawns on the European chessboard.

The regime change was hardly favorable to the Sywulkas. Emil's efforts to become naturalized had hit a brick wall. He was not loyal to Austria. As a matter of fact, he had *never* been loyal to Austria. But immigration authorities both in America and Africa still viewed him as an Austrian. As such, he would be most unwelcome in what had become British territory.

**References:**

(1)  Letter from John Snyder to Anna Marie Dahlquist, January 1984
(2)  *The Alliance Weekly,* Nov. 4, 1953
(3)  Tozer, A. W. *The Tozer Pulpit,* Volume I
(4)  Letter from Marie to the AIM, August 15, 1918
(5)  Sywulka, Marie, *Workers together with Him,* p. 22
(6)  Letter from Marie to the AIM, Nov. 4, 1918
(7)  Letter from Emil to the Editor of *Inland Africa,* October 23, 1918
(8)  Letter from Marie to the AIM, Nov. 19, 1918

# CHAPTER 7
## Delays Are Not Denials
## 1919 – 1921

### *INVITATION TO HATBORO*

It was apparent that Emil couldn't immediately return to
Africa. So as early as 1918, Howard Dinwiddie suggested an
alternate area of service. The AIM owned a house in Hatboro,
Pennsylvania, near Philadelphia. Perhaps Emil and Marie could
live there and minister to people who were passing through.

Marie replied at once, inquiring about furnishings, dishes, and
linens. She wondered what was already provided in the house, and
what she might need to bring. She also hoped they could move in
the summer so the three children would get adjusted before the
school year began. (1)

It wasn't until the summer of 1919, however, that the
Sywulkas moved into the AIM house. While Emil kept up a busy
speaking schedule, Marie enrolled the children in school and
faithfully took them to the local Methodist Church on Sundays.
Eventually the family became associated with the Berachah
Church of Philadelphia. Emil also developed a close relationship
with Dr. Donald Grey Barnhouse.

### *ROBERT C. MCQUILKIN*

When the Sywulkas arrived in Hatboro, Robert McQuilkin and
his family were still occupying the AIM home. The Sywulkas
shared the house and the two families became fast friends.

**Paul, two McQuilkin girls, and Betty in Hatboro**

The McQuilkins, assigned to Kijabe, had been all set to sail to Kenya just after the signing of the Armistice. Then their ship caught fire just before they were to board! It was sunk in the harbor, and all their material possessions were lost.

The McQuilkins, at first, still hoped to get to Africa. But there was no room for them on the next boat. A third ship would not take women and children. And so it went on, month after month.

Emil found a kindred spirit in Robert McQuilkin. Both had been thwarted in their plans to get to Africa. Both were asking God to open the right doors for them. Both were committed to preaching the Victorious Christian Life. Both were men of prayer.

**Emil with Robert McQuilkin**

Not long after the Sywulkas settled into the Hatboro home, the McQuilkins moved out. God led them into a conference ministry in the United States, and a few years later used them to found Columbia Bible College in South Carolina. But the two families remained close friends over the years. Dr. McQuilkin always regarded Emil "as the truest of missionary warriors" (2) and their home was always welcome to any member of the Sywulka clan.

## *CHRIST'S HOME*

Another special contact during the Hatboro years was with "Christ's Home for Children" in Warminster. This orphanage was founded by Dr. Albert Oetinger, a medical doctor from Germany who tried to follow the principles of George Mueller. Not only did he found the Warminster orphanage, but he also opened homes for needy children in Nicaragua, Turkey and Iran. The Nicaraguan home was closed due to political instability in that country, and the homes in Turkey and Iran were destroyed by Turkish and Kurdish soldiers in a terrible 1918 massacre.

By the time the Sywulkas got acquainted with the Pennsylvania children's home, Mr. Frederick Schwab was in charge. The older "Christ's Home" boys helped on the orphanage farm; the children's needs were met through what they raised, as well as through donations of food and clothing from businesses in the Philadelphia area. Edward recalls:

> *Christ's Home was a faith orphanage . . . No doubt their emphasis on trusting God for the supply of their needs and their strong Christian testimony drew my parents to them. That was also their way of life. (3)*

From time to time, the Sywulkas attended Sunday services at Christ's Home. Strong bonds were developed as the missionaries and the orphanage leaders spent time together in prayer.

Marie, always reaching out to others, invited some of the Christ's Home girls to spend the night at the Hatboro house. It was lighted by natural gas, but the girls were familiar only with candles and kerosene lanterns. So when they went to bed, they blew out the gas lights. Fortunately Marie went by to check on them, smelled the gas, and immediately turned the lamps off and threw open the doors.

Even after Emil and Marie returned to Africa, the people at Christ's Home kept in touch with them, praying faithfully for their ministry. Christ's Home eventually added a conference ministry to the orphanage, and in 1923 they also established a retirement home for missionaries.

### EMIL GOES WEST AND MARIE GATHERS CLOTHING

In September, 1919, Emil sent a terse note from Elm Creek, Nebraska, to the AIM Home Office:

> *[I expect to be in Denver] Sept. 29—Oct. 2. After that, address Visalia, California . . . Feel led to go to California. Pray for me.*
>
> *Yours in the faith, Emil Sywulka. (4)*

Meanwhile, Marie was preparing yet another parcel for Africa. She wrote to Headquarters:

*Miss Michelson tells me that some Friends missionaries are going to British East Africa soon . . . I wonder if these friends could and would be burdened with a parcel or two containing clothing for some children under the care of Dr. Nina Maynard . . . I do not want to burden our friends, but it would mean so much to the busy doctor to have these garments. I would gladly pay all expenses connected with getting these things out . . . Mr. Sywulka is probably in California. (5)*

## FURTHER SETBACKS

Emil wondered whether God wanted to open a stateside ministry for him, as He had done for the McQuilkins. He was willing to do whatever God planned.

It had been a long time since he had applied for citizenship. One December day in 1919, a government message arrived, addressed to Emil. He was away, as usual, but Marie opened it with high hopes. The message was not what she wanted to hear:

*In reply to your letter requesting verification of landing for Emil Sywulka, I beg to advise you that the collector of customs, who has in his custody all records of passenger arrivals prior to June 15, 1897, certifies to this office as follows:*

*The name Emil Sywulka fails to appear on the passenger list of any steamship which made entry into this port from Liverpool Nov. 18th to 30th inclusive 1882.*

Marie copied the letter by hand and sent it to the AIM headquarters with this comment:

*I rather think that I know why the name "Emil" does not appear. I remember my husband's mother saying one day, "Emil's name is really John Emanuel, but he has never gone by that name."*

*Trusting and praying that every closed door will open wide soon. "God is able."*

*I remain, yours to help save Africa with Jesus,*

*Mrs. Emil Sywulka (6)*

## LANGUAGE TEACHING

When the year 1920 dawned, there still seemed no hope of getting to Africa. Emil kept on doing what he could for the AIM: praying, speaking, and getting churches in several cities to pledge support for outgoing missionaries. He still spoke of "German East Africa" even though Tanganyika had been taken by Great Britain.

Emil's citizenship application seemed to have hit a brick wall, but he found plenty to keep him busy while he waited for the slow wheels of bureaucracy to turn.

A couple of 1920 letters show that he was preparing Sukuma language lessons for missionary candidates coming through Hatboro. He wrote:

> As to my being discouraged, I am not. I only want to sense God's will and if He is closing one door in order to open another I want to enter in. To me there is only "one field", the world, and I want to be found true to my trusteeship and ambassadorship wherever I may be . . .
>
> I am looking forward with keen joy and zest to teaching the language to the German East Africa party while waiting to see what God has in mind for the future. (7)

There were some six or seven students in Emil's Sukuma class, among them William Downey and his fiancée. The Downeys profited from Emil's language lessons and later became successful career missionaries with the AIM. Their daughters Jo and Olive Downey, both now retired in Florida, also served in Africa.

## CITIZENSHIP AT LAST

The road to naturalization was neither easy nor quick. No immigration office could verify Emil's 1882 entrance into the United States. But he *could* prove that he had entered New York, with his American wife and three African-born children, in 1913. More than seven years of continuous American residence had elapsed since then. Surely by now he could become a citizen!

And so, on February 8, 1921, Emil signed citizenship papers before the appropriate authorities in Norristown, Pennsylvania. Mr.

Palmer of the AIM and Rev. Harkness of the Hatboro Methodist Church served as witnesses. Lest there should be any further confusion over the spelling of his name, Emil signed the following oath of allegiance twice, both as *Emanuel Szivulka* and as *Emil Sywulka:*

> *I hereby declare, on oath, that I absolutely and entirely renounce and abjure all allegiance and fidelity to any foreign prince, potentate, state, or sovereignty, and particularly to Austria Hungary.*

Affixed to his "Declaration of Intention" to become a citizen was a paper from the Ellis Island authorities verifying that he arrived in New York in December, 1913, on the *Cincinnati.* (8)

As a naturalized citizen, Emil now felt free to travel outside the USA. Permission to enter British East Africa, however, was still denied, due to his Austrian birth.

To his great joy, Emil soon discovered that the Portuguese weren't as anti-Austrian as the British; they *would* allow him into their colonies. He could do evangelistic work in Portuguese East Africa until the way opened once more for Tanganyika. He wrote to Mr. Trout at the AIM Home Office:

> *Enclosed please find $100 in checks and stamps which please apply toward our outgoing. In case we sever our organic connection with the mission, would you be willing to hold our money until we are ready to go? I wouldn't mind, only thought it would bear interest there as it does not here. Thus far I feel led to go to Portuguese East Africa having Tanganyika Territory (should the way open) as an ultimate objective. But Mr. Palmer does not consider it possible to go to Portuguese East Africa under the AIM as we have no work there. I received my citizenship papers yesterday and now we can better plan to go, probably in March if we can get steamship accommodations then . . . If you hear of any steamships for South Africa let me know. (9)*

Plans came together. Emil investigated costs and schedules to Mombasa, and discovered that the Capetown route would be frightfully expensive. It would be cheaper to sail to England, then across the Mediterranean and through the Suez Canal. He sent off a second letter to Mr. Trout:

*We're planning to sail either March 22 or two weeks later
from New York via Southampton, England, and then to
Mombasa . . . The cost is $131—second class to Southampton
[and] 52 English pounds including war tax to Mombasa . . .*

*Mr. Palmer thinks I better go independent to Mombasa and
then see if the Lord will open the door to Tanganyika Territory
from there. I appreciate your kindness greatly. (10)*

## RESIGNATION FROM THE AIM

On March 21, 1921, after much prayer, and with somewhat
heavy hearts, Emil and Marie mailed a letter to the Home Office:

*To the brethren of the AIM Council:*

*We present herewith our resignation as missionaries of the
Africa Inland Mission. We have been deferring the taking of
this step hoping the door would still open into our former field
of labor. Since, however, it remains closed, and seeing we can
enter Portuguese territory which is not more than touched by
missionary effort, we feel led to enter that needy field.*

*It is not easy, after almost 15 years of service with the AIM, to
do this. Our lives have been greatly enriched by blessed
fellowship with its members both here and on the field and we
cannot pay the debt we owe. We've been enriched in faith and
love and better fitted for service. We are sorry our labors were
mixed with so much of human failure.*

*But, "tho' sundered far, by faith we meet, around one common
mercy seat." We shall continue to pray that God may visit
every AIM field with a Holy Ghost revival and covet your
prayers in our behalf for the same thing as we go forth to
carry the glorious good news to the 3,000,000 perishing souls
in Portuguese East Africa.*

*Yours to fulfill the Great Commission,*

*Mr. and Mrs. E. Sywulka (11)*

The die was cast. Emil and Marie were about to sail to an unfamiliar land. There would be no kind co-workers, either black or white, at the pier to meet them when they arrived. There would be no one ready to help them arrange housing, to teach them a new language, or to help them adjust to new customs. They would have to rely on God alone.

**References:**

(1)   Letter from Marie to Howard Dinwiddie of the AIM, July 5, 1918
(2)   Cartee, Marguerite McQuilkin, *Always in Triumph,* Fleming Revell, 1956, p. 171
(3)   Letter from Edward Sywulka to Anna Marie Dahlquist, Feb. 20, 2003
(4)   Letter from Emil to James Nutchey of the AIM, Sept. 24, 1919
(5)   Letter from Marie to James Nutchey of the AIM, Oct. 2, 1919
(6)   Letter from Marie to Mr. Fletcher of the AIM, Dec. 8, 1919
(7)   Letter from Emil to Mr. Fletcher of the AIM, January 23, 1920
(8)   Emil Sywulka citizenship papers, Norristown, PA, February 8, 1921
(9)   Letter from Emil to J. J. Trout of the AIM, February 9, 1921
(10) Letter from Emil to J. J. Trout of the AIM, March 1, 1921
(11) Letter from Emil and Marie to the AIM, March 21, 1921

# CHAPTER 8
## Portuguese East Africa
## 1921 – 1923

### BACK TO AFRICA

Even though the Sywulkas were now independent
missionaries, their friends at the AIM headquarters were happy to
help arrange their return to Africa. On April 6, 1921, the Home
Office sent word to Emil that the Fabre Line had ample
accommodations for his party. (1)

Emil's "party" included two single women —Miss Tallickson
and Miss Phankuchen— whom he had recruited while speaking at
a Bible college in Boone, Iowa. The Boone Biblical College was
known for its praying people, and the two ladies were going out
primarily as prayer partners. (2)

The *Brittania* was due to sail from New York to Lisbon on
April 15. From there, the missionaries hoped to board another ship
for Africa.

When the Sywulkas reached Lisbon, however, they
experienced further delays. Emil, who never had money to spare,
found his pocketbook stretched to pay for hotel rooms and
restaurant meals. Once more he dedicated himself to waiting and
praying for God's open doors. He also found time to visit the
Lisbon Bible Society. He wrote to the AIM headquarters:

> *We arrived here safely May 19 in the evening. Cook's agent*
> *met us and informed us that the S.S. Asia on which we were to*
> *have sailed June 5 went to dry dock and would not sail until in*
> *July. I also discovered that Cook's at Philadelphia had*
> *overcharged me $155.00 so I am asking them to refund my*
> *money which they said they would do.*

*There are three or four different S.S. lines going to Africa
from here and I am going to deal directly through the
companies themselves. Cook's have been unsatisfactory in
many ways. The Union Castle Line has the Lausteffan Castle
which is due to sail about June 15. The Transportes Maritimas
has a boat sailing about June 15. The Hamburg Line (a new
line) has one sailing June 23...*

*I don't know what boat we will take. Above address (Hotel
Victoria) will reach us if mail gets here by June 15. Later
address: c/o R. Moreton, Esq., Soc. Biblica, Praca Luiz
Camoes 20, Lisbon, Portugal. (3)*

In the end, the missionaries boarded a Dutch freighter carrying
only a few other passengers. They sailed past the Rock of Gibraltar
and through the Mediterranean, until they reached the Suez Canal.
There the captain stopped briefly to allow the travelers to gaze at
the pyramids. He even gave them time to visit a museum that
displayed ancient mummies.

As the ship continued through the Suez Canal, ten-year-old
Edward developed dysentery. He became so ill that Emil and
Marie despaired of his life. All they could do was say, "Lord,
Edward is in Thy hands. If it pleases Thee to take him, we bow to
Thy will. If it pleases Thee to heal him, use him for Thy glory."

The voyage continued into the Gulf of Aden and then out into
the Indian Ocean and into a terrible monsoon. Waves were high,
sailing was slow, and many passengers were frightfully seasick.
Day after day, the ship followed Africa's eastern coastline. The
Sywulkas crossed the equator, then sailed past the familiar port of
Mombasa. They continued their voyage past Dar-es-Salaam and
their beloved Tanganyika, and on down the long coast of
Portuguese East Africa until they reached Beira far to the south.

## BEIRA

By the time the missionaries reached Beira, Edward had
recovered from his illness, and all were glad to disembark after the
two-month voyage from America. (4)

A few days later, Emil composed a general letter:

*Beloved Fellow Laborers in the Gospel—*

*Here we are in the land of our longing and prayer. Truly God has been very gracious unto us and "goodness and mercy" has followed us all along the way...*

*We got off the Steamship Heemskerk July 18 and landed in a Greek Hotel at $2.00 (reduced rate) a day. Others were full and too high for us. At this place an old haggard cat jumped on the table occasionally and sampled the food...*

*In Lisbon I had heard of a converted Roman Catholic professor being in Beira. But how was I to find this man in a city of 1416 whites (census of 1920), and 8,000 or 9,000 natives and Asiatics? Turning to a man, while walking along, I said, "Do you know Sinhor Luz?" "Yes," said he, "he lives right here around the corner."*

*I found he was the man... We were invited to his home where tea was served us. As we bowed our heads to ask the blessing, I could hardly pray to think that our Father would give us friends the very first day in a strange land!*

*We inquired about renting a house or rooms but were assured that that was impossible. Even our friend Mr. Luz said there were no rooms to rent... But God was not going to leave us orphans... On the third day, the manager of the hotel told us of his own accord that he had a house of three rooms which he would rent us until the end of August for $40 a month...*

*We're a bit crowded... but then God has sufficient grace. The large room serves for a bedroom for the five of us. Then when we get up, the cots are folded and it is a sitting room. A table is brought in and set and lo, it is a dining room. Thank God, it is also a prayer room. God has been doing some searching and cleansing...*

*We do not know under what conditions we may do missionary work. We went to see the governor. He sent us to the intendent. He in turn sent us back to see the governor and now we are to go see the High Commissioner at Lorenco Marques. Meanwhile we have been giving out tracts in Portuguese, English, Jewish, Arabic, Hindu, Urdu, Spanish and Japanese; and also, in broken Portuguese, testifying to our Lord Jesus Christ. Have also been able to speak to some Arabs in Swahili...*

*Hundreds of natives pass by here every day. They have never heard the Gospel in their own tongue. Pray with us that this closed door may open soon. In Angola where hundreds of native schools had been closed, missionaries are now allowed to preach two days in a place in the native tongue. But they are not yet allowed to teach. God can open this door too. The most essential and the most potential ministry is "praying in the Holy Ghost." It is also the most expensive... Pray for us. (5)*

After a few weeks, the missionary party found a larger house in a better location. There was a bedroom for the two single ladies and one for Marie and Betty. Emil and his sons slept in the living room, putting up the camp cots every night and taking them down in the morning. The only drinking water came from a large tank that filled up whenever it rained; clothes had to be washed in the slightly saline water from a nearby well.

**Beira – 1921: Emil and Marie are in the center, with Miss Tallickson to the left and Miss Phankuchen to the right. Edward, Betty and Paul are in the front.
The others are members of Emil's Bible class.**

Emil found that being an independent missionary was not altogether easy. The local government was strongly opposed to Protestant missionary work, so it was hard to get permission to preach. Without belonging to any mission or church association, it was difficult to know how or where to channel new converts into churches where they could be nurtured. But Emil threw himself into evangelism and teaching wherever he found opportunity. He even started a Bible class for Chinese immigrants, just as he had done in Akron.

The Sywulkas enrolled their children in a Portuguese school taught by a strict male teacher who kept order with the aid of a large ruler. Paul and Edward shared a desk, but it was hard for them to learn their lessons when they didn't understand much Portuguese.

## MANJACAZE

Then a door opened at Manjacaze, in Gaza, one of the southernmost provinces of Portuguese East Africa. Here the Sywulkas found themselves on a mission station that had been started by a Pentecostal group. The family was provided with "a five room house"—actually four round huts surrounding and joined to a center hut.

There was ample opportunity for Emil to minister to people's spiritual needs, for Marie to minister to their medical needs, and for the two lady "prayer warriors" to uphold them before the Lord. Spiritual darkness was as great in Manjacaze as anywhere else in Africa, and workers were as scarce.

Here Emil invited local men into the home just to listen to them talk and ask them questions. Thus he began to master Shangaan, a Bantu language structurally related to Kikuyu and Sukuma, which he already knew. Within four months, Emil was preaching in the Shangaan tongue.

Manjacaze was saturated with snakes, scorpions, centipedes and virulent mosquitoes. Miss Phankuchen suffered the chills and favors of malaria for eight months without respite. When Marie offered her quinine, she replied time and again, "No, thank you. I'm trusting the Lord to heal me." Finally she agreed to take the little pills; and soon her health improved. Eventually she returned to the States, and Miss Talickson moved to South Africa, where she gave many years of service.

## BOARDING SCHOOL

The following year, Emil took his children by train to South Africa for their schooling. The plan was to enroll them in a German Lutheran school in Natal, where educational standards were somewhat higher than in the Portuguese schools they had been attending.

A German pastor met Emil and his children at the train station in Graytown, then took them in his horse-drawn buggy to the school, an hour's drive away. Nestled among eucalyptus trees, the school was close to wonderful spots for Saturday hiking and fishing, even though it was an hour's ride away from the railway station and half an hour's walk from Orange Siding, where the mail was picked up.

Emil got the children settled in their dorms, and learned more about what the school had to offer. Some classes were held in English, others in German or Dutch, and Sunday services were entirely in German.

## SAD NEWS FROM HOME

In early 1922, Emil learned that his father Peter passed away in California. His funeral service was held in Visalia's Methodist Church and the newspaper honored him as "a well known rancher." Emil's heart went out to his hard-working mother. Now a widow, she would have to work even harder. (6)

## SWAZILAND

Toward the end of 1923, Emil became ill. It seemed necessary for him to take a long rest in a favorable climate. He had word that his sister Hattie, back in California, was also ill. His letter to her gives no hint as to the nature of his own ailments:

*Dearest Sister Hattie,*

*It is some time since I heard of your illness and enforced separation from your home and family. We were sorry to hear this and can sympathize with you at least in measure. I felt impelled to write to you ere this but don't find time and strength for all I want to do or ought to do.*

*I have been here in the mountains of Swaziland since October 7 for a rest and change while Marie is staying in Gazaland attending to the sick and other work. The children are still at Hermansburg, Natal, and seem to like it better than at first. In a few weeks I will either go and see them or they will come here.*

*Well, this life is full of changes like the clouds in the sky and in the words of the poet, "Change and decay in all around I see, Oh Thou who changest not, abide with me." The things we see are temporal and the wells of this world run dry and do not permanently nor truly satisfy. But there are eternal things; God's Word, God's promises, God's love, God's joy, God's peace are all experimental and permanently and fully satisfying. I hope you are finding it so. This little, by-the-world-despised, bark of salvation will ride triumphantly and peacefully through any storm. May your trials be but gateways into the experience of the wondrous grace and love of God. (7)*

## PERMISSION TO ENTER TANGANYIKA

Emil's naturalization papers had enabled him to leave America, but they hadn't provided a magic key to enter the newly mandated Tanganyika Territory. Immigration laws continued to be strict and anyone with Austrian parentage was suspect. After all, the Austrians, in a sense, had started the Great War by seeking to avenge the murder of their archduke. No, the British didn't want any more trouble from Austrians!

Then at last the immigration bars were let down. The good news reached Emil while he was in Swaziland. No doubt his AIM friends at Nassa had been interceding on his behalf with the new government. After three years in Portuguese territory, he could return to his former field of service! It must have been with great joy that he opened and read the following telegram:

> *Sywulka has permission return Tanganyika if mission give credentials establish identity wire instructions. (8)*

The AIM Home Office mailed his credentials immediately, along with the following cover letter:

> *Dear Brother Sywulka:*
>
> *I am enclosing herewith your credentials as a reinstated member of the Mission but the same is being sent through to Mr. Hurlburt for his approval before being forwarded. This will delay it somewhat but we did not feel that there was any way in which we could do otherwise under the circumstances. I trust that when it reaches you it will find you in health and that the Lord will have clearly revealed Himself to you, more largely fitting you than ever before for such service as He may have for you to do in Tanganyika. (9)*

Emil couldn't return immediately. For one thing, his children were still in boarding school, although they would soon be released for Christmas vacation. Emil debated whether to go to them, or have them come to Swaziland to be with him. In the end, he decided on the latter course. From Swaziland, he wrote to his son Paul on December 6, 1923:

> *My Dear Paul... I'll be waiting for you at Barberton Tuesday Dec. 18th as you have planned. Get school fare if at all possible—if not get holiday return tickets... Don't spend more than necessary on the way but get meals on the train if you need it. Don't forget to thank your teachers for their labors on your behalf. I don't know if you should bring all books along. I leave that to your judgment. Do not bring those bows and arrows. (10)*

A few days later Emil wrote to his sisters Jeanette and Louise in California:

> *I have been here since October 7. Found I had to stop work for a while although I've been somewhat busy here working on a system of Bible lessons, having in view especially the needs of our native Christians. They have so very little to help*

*them. I have perhaps a third or a half of them finished. Marie stayed in Gazaland to carry her end of the work.*

*Next Thursday the children are due to arrive here. It's nearly a year they have been away. The boys, I think, did well but Betty was homesick a good bit. Marie will probably not be able to get here for Christmas.*

*We have our credentials to return to Tanganyika, our former field of labor, and probably will start for there soon if all goes well. This will make it possible for the children to go to school at Kijabe. If our children get degrees from all the schools they've attended, they'll surely have a good many!*

*May the coming year be a good year for you. May self be crucified and Christ live in you. Only Christ, though the Holy Spirit, can live a holy life. He needs, however, a human life as His dwelling place. Am enclosing some tracts which I read the other night and enjoyed much. (11)*

In 1924, after three years in what is now Mozambique, the Sywulka family returned to Tanganyika. But Emil would forever keep Portuguese East Africa close to his heart. He never stopped praying for that needy land, and he harbored a secret hope that, some day, one of his sons would be called there to take up the work.

Forty-one years after Emil was called to "the Glory Land," as he liked to call it, the AIM expanded into Mozambique. Dick Anderson tells of Don Potocki's arrival in Beira:

*On 7 December 1985, AIM's first missionary entered Mozambique in a little yellow Volkswagen. (12)*

God was answering Emil Sywulka's prayers.

---

**References:**

(1)  Letter from the AIM to Emil, April 6, 1921
(2)  Letter from Edward Sywulka to Anna Marie Dahlquist, Feb. 20, 2003
(3)  Letter from Emil to the AIM, May 21, 1921
(4)  Interview with Edward Sywulka, August 1983
(5)  Circular letter from Emil, August 2, 1921
(6)  *Visalia Times Delta,* October 21, 1922

(7)   Letter from Emil to his sister Hattie, Nov. 27 1923
(8)   Telegram to Emil Sywulka, undated
(9)   Letter from the AIM to Emil, Nov. 17, 1923
(10) Letter from Emil to his son Paul, Dec. 6, 1923
(11) Letter from Emil to his sisters, Dec. 15, 1923
(12) Anderson, Dick. *We Felt Like Grasshoppers*, Crossway, 1994, p. 304

# CHAPTER 9
## Lohumbo
## 1924 – 1930

The Sywulkas found their former field of labor greatly changed. German East Africa had become Tanganyika Territory. English was now the official language, trading was done in shillings, new roads had been opened, and some people were even traveling in automobiles.

The Sywulka family itself had changed. Paul and Edward were preschoolers, and Betty just a baby, when the family left Africa a decade before. Now the Sywulka boys were strapping teenagers, ready for studies at Rift Valley Academy in Kijabe. And Betty was already eleven.

The Sukuma simple way of life, however, was largely unchanged. The war had caused untold devastation, but most of the Sukuma area was spared from direct fighting. Even the tree-lined roads of Mwanza were left intact.

The primary foes of the Sukuma people continued to be alternating drought and floods, swarms of locusts, and beasts of prey. As they had done for centuries, people struggled just to grind out enough grain for their daily *bugali*. Their main loyalty continued to be, not to the new British government, but to their local chiefs and to their tribal king, a man named Wamba who lived in the Shinyanga district.

The Sywulkas were thrilled to see that the AIM work among the Sukuma had expanded during their ten-year absence. For a time, the Great War had reduced the missionary team to three: the Maynards and Gertrude Bowyer at Kola Ndoto (Busia). But by

1924, churches had grown, new stations had been established, and missionary numbers were again on the increase.

## LOHUMBO

William Maynard opened an outstation at Lohumbo in 1917, while British and German troops were still clashing to the south in Tabora. Lohumbo was deep in the heart of Tanganyika, 150 miles to the south of Mwanza, on beyond the stations at Kijima and Busia. It was in the Shinyanga District, on the southern borders of the Sukuma tribe.

In 1922, the AIM assigned Tom and Margaret Marsh to live at Lohumbo on a more permanent basis. Twenty-seven baptized believers and thirteen new converts awaited them. For three months, the Marshes and their baby lived in a twelve-by-twelve hut while a more permanent home was erected. (1)

The mission station was somewhat out of the way and had no modern conveniences, not even a post office. Once or twice a month, the Lohumbo missionaries sent a courier to the city of Shinyanga for their mail; each time it took the man three days to go to the city and return with a full mail pouch. To get staples such as flour, the missionaries had to send porters even farther to the city of Tabora, a six-day round trip for the men.

When the Sywulkas returned to Tanganyika as reinstated AIM missionaries in 1924, they were assigned to the Lohumbo station. From here Emil set out on long evangelistic safaris, and here he engaged in local preaching and teaching when he was home. Marie devoted herself to family duties and dispensary work, for there was no shortage of villagers with broken bones, hunting wounds, and strange illnesses.

The village of Lohumbo was surrounded by a wall of closely planted thorn bushes, intended to keep lions and hyenas out. Every night the hyenas could be heard howling as they roamed the area.

The Sywulkas lived in a four-room house with a thatched roof. Its windows had no glass panes, but rather wooden shutters which were manipulated by pulling a rope. Marie's dispensary was only a five-minute walk away, and the church building was even closer.

## TRANSLATION TEAM

When the Sywulkas arrived at Lohumbo, they found Tom
Marsh spending every possible moment working on the Sukuma
New Testament translation. Emil had revised the Church
Missionary Society's Gospel of John a decade earlier. Now he
joined the new translation team.

There were other collaborators. Zakaliya Balele was "a much-
used man of God who sometimes held an audience spellbound for
two hours as he quoted large portions of the Word, from Genesis to
Revelation. His preaching was powerful, and no sermons were
ever more eloquent than those of this man who loved the
Scriptures so dearly." (2)

Lazaro Kihayile was also part of the translation team. And so
was William Downy, who had studied Sukuma with Emil in
Hatboro. It was Mr. Downy who typed the final draft before the
Sukuma New Testament was mailed to the British and Foreign
Bible Society in London; Emil never even owned a typewriter.

## FAREWELL TO PAUL

As 1924 drew to a close, Paul, barely sixteen, left Rift Valley
Academy in Kenya, to pursue his education at Wheaton Academy
in the USA. There he would be able to get the advanced high
school subjects, which were not offered in Kenya at that time. Emil
and Marie weren't able to see him off at the Mombasa dock, and
he knew they wouldn't be able to help him financially once he got
to the States. Marie wrote:

> *My dearest Paul... I imagine that you are somewhere in the*
> *Mediterranean at this time. I trust that you are having a very*
> *delightful voyage. We do miss you... Papa has been sick with*
> *fever for a week but is off for Busia this morning as the new*
> *church is to be dedicated tomorrow... Edward wants to build*
> *a new rabbit pen today. The buckie is still here and... very,*
> *very devoted to Betty. (3)*

Emil, busy at Busia for the church dedication, also had a
message for his oldest son:

93

*My dear Paul, I came here Saturday for the dedication of the
new church. It was full yesterday and we had a good day.
Expect to start home tomorrow—part way per motorcycle. I
got the mail from Shinyanga this morning and among it were
your two letters—one from Kijabe and another from
Mombasa—the first word we have from you since leaving us.
My citizenship papers came all right. Am glad you got through
with everything and are off. I imagine you are somewhere in
the Mediterranean at this time... I had two very good meetings
the last two Sundays at Lohumbo—many Christians confessing
their sins as stealing and lying etc. I am longing to see a real
revival from heaven sent. (4)*

### SUKUMA NEW TESTAMENT

In late 1925 the Marshes left for furlough, stopping in London
to pick up a complimentary copy of the New Testament, hot off the
press. Now the Sukuma people, more than a million strong, would
have—not just Gospel portions—but the entire New Testament in
their language.

Tom in London and Emil in Lohumbo were both thrilled.
However, no sooner had they seen and handled the little volume—
the fruit of so much labor—than each of them realized it was
already in need of revision. There was yet much more work ahead.
And there was the whole Old Testament still waiting!

With the Marshes on furlough, Emil took over Tom's work:
oversight of churches and schools, along with Old Testament Bible
translation whenever he could spare a few hours. Marie found
more than enough to do, both in the dispensary work and the
Lohumbo boarding school for African girls.

### GIRLS' HOME

While at Boone Biblical College in the USA, Emil not only
enlisted two single women for Portuguese East Africa; he also
recruited two for the AIM: Isabel (Belle) Severson and Martha
Jorgensen, a native of Norway. Miss Jorgensen spent her entire
missionary career in medical work at Dr. Maynard's hospital in
Kola Ndoto (Busia), while Miss Severson joined the Sywulkas at

Lohumbo. She was put in charge of the Girls' Home, a boarding school established about 1925 or 1926. At first, only a few girls attended, but the work grew rapidly. By 1929, Emil reported:

> *Twelve were baptized at our May meeting and four new catechumens were received. We have adopted the practice of delaying receiving them for a period of two months or more to discover, first, as far as is possible, whether they are real believers... One of the four received, a young woman, has attested her faith by suffering intense persecution and shameful abuse at the hands of her relatives who at length thrust her out, deprived her of all her clothes except a small old piece of cloth to cover her loins. Someone then gave her a cloth to cover herself with. She came to us and found a place of welcome in the Girls' Home where she seems happy. The Girls' Home, by the way, is growing and will soon need to lengthen its cords. The girls that have been in my Notation class for about two years can sing well and it is a delight to hear them sing. (5)*

### EVANGEL PRESS

Another venture in the Lohumbo days was the establishment of a printing press. In 1913, Emil had used a small hand press to print John's Gospel in Sukuma, but he longed for something more efficient. True to his convictions against soliciting funds, he never mentioned his desire, but he and Marie kept praying about it. Marie recalled later:

> *For a long time we sensed the need of a printing press for the furtherance of the Gospel. This real need was not broadcast, but presented at the Throne of Grace: "Lord, supply us with a good press to the praise of Thy glory." Then one day a letter was received from two ladies in Oregon, informing us that funds were being sent to us to purchase a press!*

> *In due time the press reached the field. Instead of being brought to Lohumbo, it was put off at Tinde, about thirteen miles away. The rainy season was on, and the station superintendent away on a long safari. So we women had to act. No door at Tinde was wide enough to get the press through and under shelter. Miss Severson made several trips to Tinde on her bicycle to see what could be done. Finally we*

*got the service of a team of oxen and a wagon from an Indian.
It seems everyone helped—Indian, white and black, heathen,
Muslim, Christian—and the press landed at Lohumbo in spite
of the fact that one of the oxen decided to lie down and not
work. (6)*

## LETTERS TO PAUL

From 1925 on, Marie (and to a lesser extent Emil) kept up a regular correspondence with Paul, who was in the United States.

Paul carefully kept his parents' letters and, in time, he kindly shared them. The following excerpts from Marie's letters to her son, composed between Easter of 1926 and Easter of 1929, tell the story of the Lohumbo years and reveal some of her own struggles and joys:

*You must have had a good Easter Day yesterday... Papa
expected to be at Nassa yesterday. So none of my family were
here. I had the Lohumbo bunch in for supper Saturday night.
This was my Easter offering. One can give in so many ways.
(7)*

*I suppose Papa will be coming home on the Feb. 5th boat. I
am so glad that he could have this much needed change. He
has been working very hard and there is plenty of hard work
ahead of him when he gets home. Isn't it wonderful how the
Lord has undertaken for your father's health after that severe
breakdown in South Africa? I knew that the Lord would
undertake for He had told me that He was going to get us back
to Tanganyika and He wouldn't send a dead man up here . . .*

*I had just been in the garden a few minutes yesterday when it
began to thunder in the distance. The boys said, "The rain is
very near," and directly big drops began to fall, though the
sun was shining brightly. Anyway I hurried home fast as I
could. The sun did not shine long after that and the wind
began to blow just awful. The rain seemed to come in great
horizontal sheets instead of just from above. I thought of our
grass roofs when I heard the tin roof blowing off Miss
Severson's kitchen. The storm was so blinding that one could
not see far. As soon as we could we went out to see the
damage done—quite a lot of grass is off our roof letting in the
sunshine and rain...*

*Some of the big trees near the house have big branches broken off. Grass strewn everywhere. The little girls cried, "House on fire," and at first I thought they meant the Girls' Home but it was the nice big new hut off to the north past the girls' house; lightning did the work. The worst part of that is that a poor deaf and dumb half-wit was in the hut and got terribly burned because he did not know enough to get out even with help. They brought him here, he is mostly bandages from head to waist, awful burns on his arms from shoulder to finger tips. The skin off, most of his back and face burned. My heart certainly bleeds for the poor fellow.*

*As to the kitchen roof, rafters and all went off... scattered about like straws. Two of our girls and one of the babies got out of the kitchen just in time. We are so full of praise to our Father that there has been no loss of life and limb. I rallied some of our men together and the roofing was put on. There are lots of papai on the ground, aloe trees and banana plants... I expect to do a dressing pretty soon so must hasten to a close. (8)*

*Papa's paper, "Messenger of the Kingdom", is not all bad. Maybe I told you that we do not have enough type, that is, certain letters, which are required so many more times in Sukuma than in English. An "n" turned upside down makes a fairly good "u." Most folks would have given up the job for a while. Not your father, though.*

*While at the dispensary today word came that a leopard had taken a little girl a couple of miles from here . . . Said she was badly torn all over her little body. Of course she did not live. Poor little child .*

*Our old kitchen is torn down (before it could fall down) and a small stick and mud building put up to answer for a kitchen until we can build one during the dry season if the Lord wills. (9)*

*I have two more interesting surgical cases. One man was badly speared in the shoulder. The spear had been given a twist and a turn, that makes a nasty sore... then a boy was brought from the king's with a compound fracture of the forearm. The school boys were playing leap frog and he got hurt. I was just up [from an illness] and felt I did not have the*

97

*strength to undertake the case, but asked the Lord to
undertake. To my surprise I found that the king and helpers
had pulled the bone in place. I put a little dressing over the
place where the bone had come through, used three little reeds
for splints, and tied up the arm... Probably the king has had a
first aid lesson at Shinyanga or Tabora. I understand two men
died at Busia that had been mauled by a lion... I have a boy
about fourteen here that cannot get well. He has had kidney
trouble and his face especially is so bloated that his eyes are
almost shut. Am glad that I can make him a little more
comfortable if not cure him. (10)*

*I find myself looking forward to Easter. My, wouldn't I enjoy
hearing good Easter music. I hope you will enjoy some of it
for me ... I always miss you children so much on special days.
If this reaches you before Mothers Day, then send something
to Grandma for me. A letter or card maybe. Don't forget to
write to Aunt Anna now and then. It will do her heart good.
She has been a very good sister to your mother. (11)*

**1929 missionary conference: Emil at far left, Marie seated in front of him.
The children are Marshes and Hesses.**

**The same conference. Tom Marsh is standing fourth from left
and Margaret Marsh is seated second from right.**

## *FLORENCE TILLEY*

During the Sywulkas' prolonged first furlough, Emil had
recruited half a dozen or more new missionaries. Besides the four
women from Boone Biblical College, there was Laura
Thompson—noted AIM teacher and writer—and Florence Tilley.

Florence never forgot the day when Emil looked into her eyes
and said, "I believe God is calling YOU to Africa." She heeded the
call and joined the work at Lohumbo. Much later, she recalled how
Emil met her at the boat, took her shopping for staples in Mwanza,
and then admonished her: "Miss Tilley, if you ever have a financial
need, don't mention it to anyone except the Lord. Remember that
He says: 'I am the Lord and my glory will I not give to another.'"

When Florence failed to receive the support which her home
church had pledged, she remembered Emil's admonition and told
no one of her need. Month after month went by, and still there
were no checks from America. Except for flour, most of her staples
ran out; she lived on bread and on tomatoes from her garden.

Sometimes Marie, unaware of the situation, sent over baked
goodies. And one time a little African boy brought some milk as a
gift.

99

In time, Florence's church discovered that their treasurer had been absconding with the missionary's support funds! The matter was set right, and checks started coming once again, but Florence never forgot Emil's admonition to trust God alone without letting others know her needs, for He had said: "I am the Lord and my glory will I not give to another." (12)

For years, Florence served at the Lohumbo Girls' School. Later, when the Sywulkas opened the Mwanza station, she was transferred to that city and once again became their close co-worker. There God used her mightily in a teaching ministry and in developing Bible curriculum especially suited to Africa's needs. Decades later, in a letter to a granddaughter, Marie praised Florence:

> *She is a dear, dear friend and co-worker. And has shown me many, many kindnesses down the years. For some years she has been in charge of the Bible Club work out here and not in vain. Long years ago I remember your Grandfather Sywulka saying, "I wish we had a hundred like her." (13)*

## GOODBYE TO EDWARD

Emil and Marie had said farewell to Paul in 1924. Now, in 1928, it was time to say goodbye to Edward.

Providentially, Theodore and Josephine Westervelt, former members of the AIM, invited Edward to live with them in the United States. They had left Africa for health reasons but were providing a home for teenage "missionary kids" in Siloam Springs, Arkansas.

The boys—about a dozen of them—formed a musical band and performed in churches where the Westervelts spoke. When fall came, they enrolled in John Brown College. Edward had attended Rift Valley Academy at Kijabe, but he had not graduated. Nevertheless, Mrs. Westervelt felt he was fully ready for college, and she made sure he was accepted at John Brown. Later, when the Westervelts moved to Columbia, South Carolina, Edward transferred to Columbia Bible College.

## A GROWING MINISTRY

In a circular letter to supporters, Marie tried to summarize the events of 1928. So much had happened! Africa's relentless fevers had again attacked both her and Emil. She no doubt recalled Frank Millen's grave at Kijima; Frank had died from the blackwater fever, while Emil, also far from medical facilities, had survived the same dread scourge.

But even more than giving praise to God for restored health, Marie wanted to let their USA friends know how the work was growing:

*It is a little over a year that the Field Council voted that the Sywulka family go home and furlough and naturally we had hoped to see some of you face to face before this, but the way did not open. So we praise God for another year of service . . .*

*The first of last year found me fighting repeated attacks of Spirillum fever, and in July Mr. Sywulka went to the very verge of the grave with blackwater fever two hundred miles from home and only native loving hearts and black hands to minister to his needs until help came.*

*We have much to thank God for... There are sixteen girls in the Home at present. All are very busy in their gardens, this being the Rainy Season. Generally speaking they are nice girls. We trust that their being here for training will mean better wives and mothers in coming days as well as a strong Christian womanhood among Africa's degraded women.*

*Our school is under Miss Tilley's charge. Miss Tilley is a young and new missionary and, we think just splendid... A few steps farther on will bring you to the place where Genesis is being printed on the Evangel Press. Rejoice with us that our people are going to have Genesis in their own language. Not a subtracted version but all of it as God saw fit to give it to mankind.*

*While writing several little folks came in—Edith Bates, the one white child on the station, some of the [mixed race] children that we are caring for, and several real Africans—all brimful of mischief and running over!... We suggest that they play in the shade out under the trees, for we have a patient in the next room who is ill... Dear African babies, lovely blossoms in my heartsease garden.*

*In the dispensary there were nearly five thousand cases the past year. This part of the work never takes a vacation... however, our gracious Lord never fails us. How wonderfully He has helped us over and over again. To Him all the praise! (14)*

## GENESIS IN SUKUMA

While Marie handled roughly 5,000 medical cases a year, Emil was printing Genesis on the Evangel Press. He wrote to Paul:

*For some days we have been working on a stand for holding type boxes. This morning I started Filipo (the lame fellow) on cleaning and sorting the type... Expect to do some printing soon. Yesterday we received our new song books and first Readers. Maybe I am not delighted? They're a good job and will meet a very great need. (15)*

Later, Marie recorded simply that in 1929 Genesis was "printed by Evangel Press, on our Lohumbo Station." (16)

### RETURNING AND RESTING AT NASSA

Both Emil and Marie were weary, and there were no funds in hand for the furlough that the mission had granted them. When Marie was given an opportunity to go to Nassa for a few days of rest, she jumped at the chance. She was able to go the whole way by auto, thanks to some friends who were driving! From Lohumbo, they went to Busia, then to Nera, then through Mwanza and finally sixty more miles to Nassa. From her former mission station, Marie wrote to Paul:

*How different from the olden days when I walked to and from Mwanza, sixty miles! Mwanza is getting to be a very important place on the map since the railroad terminates there. You know one can get on the train at Dar-es-Salaam and go through to Mwanza. Well, it seems good to be at Nassa again. When we left for USA I said to the people here, "We will be back in a year." The one year has been multiplied by*

*sixteen!... It is quiet and restful here and the lake breeze is
very refreshing. I'll have to fess up to being very tired. This is
my first vacation in nearly three years... It does seem that you
children ought to be here. You running about busy at play with
Anna and Eva. Edward busy eating dirt by the handful and
running outdoors under the tropical sun without his helmet.
Betty, a baby in my arms... I thank my Father for all these
happy memories. (17)*

### "WE ARE ON OUR WAY"

The stock market crash in the USA made the possibility of
furlough seem even more remote, but by early 1930, funds were in
hand for passage to America. Marie wrote to Paul from Victoria,
Tanganyika:

*Here we are on our way to Kijabe. As soon as we know about
booking we will let you know. Your father wants to take the
South Africa route to get a much needed rest and see his
numerous friends along the coast... The whole Mwanza
church saw us off at Mwanza and presented us with dozens of
mangoes and oranges. (18)*

### MURDER!

Just before Emil and Marie reached Kijabe, they heard some
horrifying news. Hulda Stumpf, a missionary on that station, had
been murdered in her own bed, her body brutally battered, on the
first night of the new year—1930. No one seemed to know who
had done the terrible deed, nor why. The Kenya missionaries could
not have foreseen that this atrocity would be just a prelude to the
horrors of the Mau Mau rebellion. For a strong anti-white
sentiment was already sweeping through Kenya.

When they reached Kijabe, Marie wrote to Edward:

*Here we are at Kijabe and enjoying it except that I had three
days of fever and Papa came down yesterday. The conference
was fine and it certainly was nice to see the older missionaries
again. I had not seen Stauffachers for years, since the oldest
boy was a boy, and then I am so glad to have met the younger
folks.*

*We all miss dear Miss Stumpf. The government is doing all it can to find the murderers. Several men are being held.*

*We leave Mombasa Feb. 3rd D.V. As we are going the southern way it will take us forty-one days to reach England. (Costs less too).*

*Betty has grown wonderfully and is such a dear girl. You will be proud of your sister when you see her...*

*I do not know just when we will see you as I want to go to Philadelphia and to Akron first. The Lord will lead. We want to be in His will and plan. (19)*

## CUFF LINKS AND A CUP AND SAUCER

From Kijabe, Emil, Marie and Betty traveled to Nairobi. There Marie splurged and bought some gold cuff links for Emil. But he refused to wear them. After she got to America, she wrote to Edward:

*Under separate cover I am sending you a Sukuma New Testament. Also a pair of cuff links which I bought in Nairobi for your father but he refused them, said there was too much gold for a preacher. He really needed the links. So I have kept them for you. (20)*

It was often thus. Marie would buy Emil a gift, and then he'd either refuse it, sell it, or give it away. Another time she told Edward that for Christmas "I gave your father a serviceable cup and saucer for daily use. I think he will keep this sort of thing and not give it away." (21)

Emil was fond of quoting his good friend Dr. Tozer: "Oh, the blessedness of possessing nothing." Not even when headed for America, with the prospect of preaching in fashionable churches, did he want material possessions or fancy clothing to weigh him down.

## References:

(1) Wadell, Ginny, *Safari Servant,* Foundry Press, Orangeburg, SC, 1980, p. 48
(2) *Ibid,* p. 54
(3) Letter from Marie to her son Paul, Dec. 5, 1924
(4) Letter from Emil to Paul, Dec. 8, 1924
(5) Circular letter from Emil, Summer 1929
(6) Sywulka, Marie, *Workers together with Him,* AIM Press, Rethy, Congo, 1954, p. 47
(7) Letter from Marie to Paul, April 5, 1926
(8) Letter from Marie to Paul, January 27, 1927
(9) Letter from Marie to Paul, March 28, 1927
(10) Letter from Marie to Paul, November 27, 1927
(11) Letter from Marie to Paul, March 22, 1929
(12) Interview with Florence Tilley, 1967
(13) Letter from Marie to granddaughter Anna Marie, March 23, 1960
(14) Circular letter from Marie, January, 1929
(15) Letter from Emil to Paul, April, 1929
(16) Sywulka, Marie, *Workers together with Him,* p. 35
(17) Letter from Marie to Paul, May 31, 1929
(18) Letter from Marie to Paul, January 17, 1930
(19) Letter from Marie to Edward, January 28, 1930
(20) Undated letter from Marie to Edward
(21) Letter from Marie to Edward, January 5, 1934

# CHAPTER 10
# Second Furlough
# 1930 – 1931

## A SCATTERED FAMILY

The Sywulkas' second furlough began with a whirlwind of meetings. The family was scattered—Paul at Wheaton College, Edward at Columbia Bible College, Marie and Betty with relatives in Akron, and Emil going west. This time, he took the Greyhound bus. He stopped briefly in Wheaton to see Paul, spoke in churches along the way to California, and finally reached his relatives there.

Letters from both Emil and Marie to their sons show their longing to have the family reunited. At times, they also reveal miscommunications and disappointments. Between the lines, one can see how little income the Sywulkas (and their relatives and supporters) had in those Depression days. And yet, a triumphant spirit of praise shines through.

## MARIE IN AKRON

Marie, with Betty in tow, started out in the home of her sister Anna Baumert. Next she moved in with her sister Lizzie Williams, and for part of the time she sent Betty to live with her brother Adam Snyder.

There seemed to be plenty to do besides hold meetings. There were relatives to visit, and dear little grand-nieces and nephews to rock to sleep. Marie was even on hand to deliver one niece's baby when the doctor didn't arrive on time! Yet she missed her husband and sons. The following excerpts from Marie's letters to Edward give us a glimpse of her Akron furlough:

*Papa left for Chicago Friday morning so I suppose that he
and Paul are having a great time these days. I suppose that
you and Papa did the same thing though I have heard very
little about it. Papa never was any good at telling me about
himself or happenings...*

*Grandma gave me a spring coat. I certainly needed it. This
was a very definite answer to prayer. I am sure the good Lord
will give Betty one too.*

*We are still here at Uncle Henry's and will probably make this
my headquarters until Paul Baumert gets home about the
middle of June. Don't know just where I will pitch my tent
after that...*

*Betty is in Central High here, "listening" as the year is too
near the close to take regular class work. I am trying to pay
for our keep here. I know the folks can hardly afford to keep
us free of charge...I told Betty the other day she might have to
go to work...*

*My throat is off and on so to speak. Fairly good for a day or
two, then bad again. I have not taken meetings but expect to
talk in Canton tomorrow. (1)*

*Yesterday I had a meeting at the Alliance Church. The Lord
was with us and blessed as He always does. They gave me ten
dollars. I do appreciate it. In the evening Betty talked at the
Young People's meeting. At the close two bills were pressed
into her hand. She thought two dollars but when she got home
it was a one and a five. I was so glad for her. These gifts meet
real needs. I have wanted a few rooms of our own so very
much but so far we have not been able to do it. Most of all I
am longing to have the family together, all of us. Again the
Lord is able.*

*I suppose that Papa is with his people by now. I know [your]
Grandma will be glad. I suppose they will find a little corner
for him somewhere. (2)*

*Betty and I are here at Aunt Lizzie's. It is much cooler here
than in town and better for us in several ways. One thing, no
rent to pay. It is so good of Aunt Lizzie to open her home. It
saves us about $30.00 a month. However I am longing for a*

107

*little corner of our own. I suppose that you are at Montrose by
this time. I trust that all will have a very profitable time.*

*Papa writes that he is coming east to attend Montrose late in
July, also Christ Home conference. I too would like to be there
but so far don't see my way clear. It costs so much to travel. I
hope that you can come here. We must get together
somewhere. Pray to that end.*

*Betty and I have been down with malaria, colds and tonsillitis.
Betty has many days when she is not well. I am glad that she is
with me. (3)*

## EMIL IN CALIFORNIA

Meanwhile, Emil had reached the West Coast. From Berkeley,
where his brother was "putting wife through school," he wrote to
Edward:

*My brother and his wife expect to start for Los Angeles and I
am going along. We'll go the coast way. Last week we went to
Yosemite Park and say, it was great. How I wished you and
Paul could have been along. Mountains! A mile high straight
up, and waterfalls many. One drop of Yosemite Falls is 1430
ft. The surroundings are so immense that distances are
deceiving. One day we climbed to the top of Nevada Falls and
another day we went to see the Mariposa Grove of the aged,
magnificent monsters of the forest. The sights are enough to
take your breath away and to make the tears come. If I have
another opportunity I will go again for there are many hikes
and climbs to take...*

*My brother and I have fine times praying together. I think a lot
of him... He is the chief cook and I am the chief bottle washer
when his wife is at school. Yesterday we washed just piles of
clothes. I got my hands clean enough to last for a whole month
if cleanliness were a perennial. (4)*

That summer, with mixed emotions, Emil wrote a tender
good-bye note to his widowed mother. He could not have known
that he would never again see her, his sisters, or his brother.

He was eager to attend conferences in Pennsylvania. Marie wrote to Edward:

> *Papa expects to start East in a few days. I rather think that he does not have quite enough money. He has not said so, only I am wondering so please pray for that. He wants to get to Montrose and Christ Home Conferences. I do not know the dates... Keep on praying too that our whole family get together in God's own time and place. Seems Paul will not be coming just now. (5)*

When Emil gleaned enough money, he bought a ticket that would take him through Chicago, then wrote asking Paul to meet him. When he arrived at the station, he looked all around, but there was no Paul.

"Well, Paul must be in Akron," he told himself, so he went on to meet Marie, but there was no Paul in Akron either! Later, he learned that his letter hadn't reached his son in time. Marie told Paul that Emil was "disappointed enough to cry" and in a letter to Edward she called the experience "a mix-up and disappointment all the way around."

Marie was disappointed, not just because Emil and Paul hadn't connected, but also because Emil wouldn't be staying long in Akron. She told Edward, "I doubt if he will stay more than a day. Wish that I was going east with him... let patience do her perfect work." (6)

## ELIADA CONFERENCE

Almost as soon as he arrived in Akron, Emil received a telegram from Robert McQuilkin. It was an invitation to speak at the Eliada Summer Bible Conference in North Carolina. So instead of heading east, Emil went south. Mary Beam, who later devoted her own life to Africa, recalls the Eliada meetings:

> *Mr. Sywulka was the speaker and came a bit late for his speaking engagement. He was covered with dust from the long trip he had made to get there—a great missionary in my estimation. Dr. Robert C. McQuilkin insisted that he come to the podium and speak just as he was. I remember I could feel some sort of groans or sighs from some in the audience who*

*included elite people from Augusta. It came through to me as
an expression from some that perhaps Dr. McQuilkin had not
been so discreet as he should have been in asking a speaker to
take the podium when he was still in his traveling clothes. The
whole atmosphere in the meeting changed soon after dear Mr.
Sywulka got into his message. By the time we got to lunch that
day, no one could find words enough to express their
appreciation for his tremendous burden of heart for his people
in East Africa and his ability to communicate it. The
impression that remains with me is that no one thought of how
he was dressed nor how he looked. (7)*

## BACK TO CHRIST'S HOME

That fall, the Sywulka boys continued their college studies:
Paul at Wheaton, and Edward at Columbia Bible College. Betty,
finishing up high school, lived with the McQuilkins in South
Carolina. For a couple of months, Emil and Marie made Christ's
Home in Warminster, Pennsylvania, their headquarters. Begun as
an orphanage, Christ's Home had added a conference center as
well as housing for furloughing missionaries. The Sywulkas had
made many friends at the home on their first furlough, and they
were warmly received once again.

Christ's Home was a godsend for the Sywulkas. Both Emil
and Marie could come and go as they pleased, taking speaking
engagements wherever doors opened. Marie's letters show that she
accepted invitations in Hatboro, Philadelphia, Newton, and
Reading. Emil, true to form, traveled farther away.

The Sywulkas enjoyed warm fellowship at Christ's Home, and
also introduced some of their co-workers to the center. Years later,
fellow-missionary Ruth Shafer wrote about her first furlough:

*It was dear Emil Sywulka who opened the way for us, a
penniless, half discouraged family of four kids (with no place
to call home, short of Chicago way out west) to come here to
this wonderful place, of all things, called CHRIST'S HOME.
We never knew how we got to come here, until the
Superintendent told us it was Emil Sywulka who recommended
our names. (8)*

All his life, Emil was an avid mountain climber. In the spiritual realm, too, he sought to attain the peaks. He believed in "life on the higher plain," and he prayed and preached revival. The following letter, written to Edward from Christ's Home, gives us insight into Emil's theology as well as his plans for that fall:

> *While we ought to be "stablished in the faith" we must not be so rigidly encased as to be impervious to new truth. Not any one person or body of people has ever held all of God's truth. It takes all the members of the body of Christ to display all the gifts and graces of the Lord. I believe the baptism with the Holy Ghost and power is not only indispensable but the great lack of God's people today, as evidenced by a general powerlessness and barrenness of life and service. Read Isaiah 35 for a picture of gospel blessing that fairly makes one's heart leap.*
>
> *I expect to leave for the west October 4 as my plans are now. Greetings to the "bunch" and to Westervelts and McQuilkins. (9)*

Emil gained a reputation, not only for his impassioned missionary appeals, but also for his "Deeper Life" messages. There were more speaking opportunities than he could handle. From Christ's Home, Marie wrote to Edward:

> *Your father started west last Saturday. He expects to be in Cleveland Thursday and in Akron over Sunday at least, then westward again. Remember Papa in much prayer. God has used his messages in a very wonderful way—to God the praise. I am still busy and trying to do some of the work Papa could not take. I want to be with you folks, but must not run away until the Lord says "Go." (10)*

Marie intended to spend some time in South Carolina with Edward and Betty, but she didn't want to leave Pennsylvania until her speaking engagements were fulfilled. Again, she wrote:

> *Keep on praying for your mother and father. We want our work to count for God. I am meeting a group of Christian nurses Oct. 25th. Wouldn't it be fine to have some of them hear God's voice calling to the foreign field. God is able. If it wasn't for some of these very important meetings I would have been with you folks before this. A letter from the Philadelphia General Hospital this morning asks me to speak to the student*

111

*body and meet the alumnae on the evening of Nov. 3rd. I feel
that this is a life-time opportunity. Not much would they give
me this opportunity if I wasn't a graduate from there and
because they want to hear about things as they are in Africa.
(11)*

By late November, Marie was with her children in South
Carolina. The McQuilkins welcomed her warmly, and the
Westervelts invited her and Betty for Thanksgiving. She wrote to
Paul:

*Betty and I are still at McQuilkins though we expect to get
settled elsewhere soon. I have rented three rooms and a bath
(first floor) for twenty-five dollars a month, heat and light
extra. This place is near the Bible College... I must order coal
today and kindling too. Getting started is expensive but we
have a rich Father and He has promised to meet all our needs.
I want to trust Him with simple childlike faith and trust. (12)*

Letters show that in December 1930, Emil was at Iowa's
Boone Biblical College. But by early 1931, he was with Marie in
South Carolina. His furlough year was up; yet he wasn't quite
ready to return to Africa. He wrote to the AIM home office:

*In regard to sailings, the dates given are a bit early for me as I
feel I ought to stay with my children a little longer. We only
had a few days together last summer... Mrs. Sywulka does not
feel she will start before July. (13)*

Marie echoed his thoughts in her own letter to the Home
Office, although she didn't share the nature of her physical
problems:

*I am taking meetings again. Mr. Sywulka is having open doors
for service too. Mr. Sywulka is still planning to go before I do.
I do so wish that we could go together... The doctor says that I
ought not to go "just yet" but I ought to be in good shape for
Africa by July. (14)*

### ORDINATION

Emil wanted to take care of one more thing before returning to
Africa. From Darby, Pennsylvania, he wrote to the AIM:

*As probably you know the marriage question in our
Tanganyika Territory field has been very loose for years, the
native Christians marrying according to native custom and
frequently, in outlying districts, marriages are contracted
which are not in accord with New Testament standards. We
are severely criticized by not a few of our fellow missionaries
of the other AIM fields, and I believe, justly so. It has been
several times decided that Christian marriage be adopted but,
thus far, only partially carried out.*

*British law requires the one who officiates to be regularly
ordained. I have ministered often here at Maranatha
Tabernacle and I believe they would ordain me. Let me know
your thoughts on the matter. (15)*

The ordination took place on April 18, 1931, in Darby. Marie,
miles away in South Carolina, could only pray for Emil.

On the Examining Council were local ministers from Baptist,
Methodist, Reformed and Presbyterian churches as well as from
the Maranatha Tabernacle and the AIM Home Office. The
secretary wrote: "It was moved that the Council declare itself fully
satisfied" and then added, "Several bore testimony to [Emil
Sywulka's] long and faithful service as a missionary. His splendid
statement of doctrine supported by the Scriptures was most
refreshing." (16)

## BACK TO AFRICA

Only six days after standing before the Examining Council,
Emil was on the high seas. Marie, who must have felt keen
disappointment at being left behind, wrote to her son Paul from
South Carolina:

*Your father left America April 24th on the* American
Merchant... *expecting to get to England May 4th. Papa had to
work very, very hard the last weeks and must have been dead
tired body and mind, so I am glad that he is getting a rest.
Folks were very good to him in giving him needed money for
personal use. We sent Papa a farewell telegram as there was
no time for another letter. (17)*

It wasn't long before she received a report from her husband. She was relieved to know that he was indeed getting a good rest— studying his Swahili New Testament, reading, walking, praying, and writing letters. He also mentioned that he found time to play "shuffle board or chess in between."

> Here we are nearing the end of the journey and I must write. Due at London docks early Monday morning so tomorrow will be a busy day. The trip has been very fine so far—hardly anyone sea sick unless it was the first day. The boat has rocked only slightly and sometimes not at all. But, of course, it takes more than that to make life blessed—peace of mind and rest of heart and fellowship of those like-minded. The passengers are all of the better class and are very nice except that they make the air blue with tobacco smoke everywhere including at meals. Most of the women, I think, smoke. I thought I would get away from that kind of a thing, but perhaps we'll have to wait till we get to heaven. The food is excellent and of a wide variety—waiters are nearly all German. Cabin is large. (18)

After a stop-over in London, Emil sailed southward. His ship docked briefly in Morocco. From here, he wrote to Edward, who was about to make a summer trip to California with the Westervelts and their young men's band:

> Well, I am glad to be on the way to dear old Africa. Walked around on its soil today at Ceuta, Morocco, a city of 54,000. But oh, what a desert spiritually and morally. Corruption and degradation written on all faces except the children's. I inquired carefully as to any gospel witness. It seems there is none. Roman Catholics exert little influence and Islam has only a small mosque up on a hill. Where are the laborers? Need! Opportunity! Urgency! Here it is. Probably over half of the ship's passengers took an excursion on a primitive-looking train to Tetuan, a Moorish town 43 kilometers from here. I walked through the town (Ceuta). We left at 5 p.m. and soon were passing Gibraltar but the direct rays of the evening sun prevented us from seeing it clearly.
>
> In London I visited the All Nations Bible School. They have 25 students. Seventy have gone to all parts of the world since it was started by F. B. Meyer and others eight years ago. They have a most beautiful 20-acre estate laid out by an Italian in

*1834. The penalty for coming late to meals is to shake hands
with the principal. I came late once but was not required to
shake hands for which I was glad of course. I also visited the
Colony nearby. They have about the same number of students
and live army style. Fenton Hall who died in South America
was from there. I will send his biography to Paul. It is that of
a real hero...*

*"The steps of a good man are ordered of the Lord, and he
delighteth in his way." May this be true of your Western trip.
Don't fail to notify, and if possible visit, your kith and kin in
Denver, Los Angeles and Berkeley.*

*Greet the "bunch," including the Westervelts and also my
friend Mr. Smith.*

*Be sure to climb Half Dome in Yosemite National Park.*

*Perhaps mother can send you some money for the way. I don't
know how she will come out financially. Goodbye. (19)*

The ship continued on its way through the Mediterranean.
From the port of Genoa, Emil wrote again to his wife. His positive
reaction to Mussolini's Italy is certainly interesting in view of later
world events, which Emil could not possibly have foreseen:

*My dear Marie—We docked here about 3:30 p.m. today, and
leave for Port Said tomorrow at 12. Many passengers received
letters on board ship but there was none for me.*

*I wonder where you are by now—at Akron? I'll address your
letter there. Today is Sunday but there was no service outside
of the Church of England one at 7:30 a. m. There's a bunch of
us missionaries—3 A.I.M., 3 Universities, 3 Berliners, 3
Roman Catholic sisters, and there are more German
missionaries coming tomorrow.*

*Everything is clean and law and order here. I certainly would
like to take off my hat to Mussolini. Our cabins were left open
in perfect security. The dock porters came on board and
carried all the passengers' baggage to the railroad station
absolutely without tips, no beggars around and everything
seems to bristle with energy. Mussolini's in the city today and
the city and ships are full of flags, ours included. Agile, alert,*

*smart-looking young soldiers everywhere. This change is welcome. Marseilles was disgusting... talk about a dirty town!*

*I suppose my last letter will be from Port Said as the boat does not stop at Aden and I won't wish to write from Mombasa. I'll know when I get the mail at Dar-Es-Salaam.*

*I trust these remaining days for you will be fruitful and delightful. Greet Baumerts and the rest, and all the friends. Offer to pay Baumerts for sending my helmet to Brooklyn.*

*Faithfully your husband, Emil (20)*

On June 22, 1931, Emil reached Dar-Es-Salaam. The Kijima missionary conference was only two weeks away. He wondered whether he'd be re-assigned to Lohumbo, or whether the field council had a new station in mind for him. Wherever God might lead, he was willing to go.

### References

(1) Letter from Marie to Edward, May 11, 1930
(2) Letter from Marie to Edward, May 26, 1930
(3) Letter from Marie to Edward, July 11, 1930
(4) Letter from Emil to Edward, June 6, 1930
(5) Letter from Marie to Edward, July 15, 1930
(6) Undated letter from Marie to Edward
(7) Letter from Mary Beam to Pauline Sywulka, August 2001
(8) Undated letter from Ruth Shaffer to Donald and Judy Shoff
(9) Letter from Emil to Edward, Sept. 23, 1930
(10) Letter from Marie to Edward, Oct. 8, 1930
(11) Letter from Marie to Edward, Oct. 16, 1930
(12) Letter from Marie to Paul, Nov. 11, 1930
(13) Letter from Emil to the AIM, Feb. 25, 1931
(14) Letter from Marie to the AIM, March 23, 1931
(15) Letter from Emil to the AIM, April 10, 1931
(16) Ordination papers for Emil Sywulka, April 18, 1931
(17) Undated letter from Marie to Paul
(18) Letter from Emil to Marie, May 5, 1931
(19) Letter from Emil to Edward, May 26, 1931
(20) Letter from Emil to Marie, May 31, 1931

# CHAPTER 11
## Mwanza
## 1931 – 1932

### *ANNUAL CONFERENCE*

Each year, the AIM missionaries looked forward to conference time. Often physically weary and emotionally drained, they gathered to renew their strength. It was a time of extended prayer, inspirational messages, bonding with fellow workers, and conducting mission business.

Preceding the missionaries' conference was the "Native Conference" where African pastors and teachers gathered to report on their year's work in the outstations, to fellowship together, and to hear helpful Bible messages.

The "Native Conference" for 1931 was scheduled to begin June 27; the missionary conference on July 1. Emil was eager to attend both sessions and to learn where the Field Council would assign him. Marie, far away in America, wrote:

> *I suppose that the Council met and decided what to do with us.*
> *I hope to know in two or three weeks. At least before I sail so*
> *as to address the boxes properly. (1)*

### *NEW ASSIGNMENT*

Before the conferences were over, Emil learned that he was to open a new station—this time in Mwanza. He wrote to his family from Kijima:

> *Here I am once more, in the land of need and therefore of*
> *responsibility—a debtor to share God's free, wondrous grace.*
> *Our boat reached Dar Es Salaam June 22 and I arrived at*
> *Malampaka June 26 before daybreak... I didn't want to hire a*

*truck... so I started the 36 miles here by leg-a-mobile... Within five miles of Kijima one of my old friends caught up with bicycle and immediately insisted on my taking it, which I did gladly for I was beginning to get blisters on my feet.*

*On arrival I was, of course, greeted and serenaded and kingshish-ed on all sides. And I'm certain I didn't buy their friendship with shillings. The Christians in Mwanza and round about, in anticipation of my coming, have bought and fixed up a house for me at a cost of 190 shillings. At our Field Council Meeting a few days ago it was decided to "open Mwanza station with Mr. Sywulka in charge." How I wish you, Paul, were here now to superintend the building. I will, however, endeavor to get competent native builders...*

*Monday the Marsh family and I are going to select a site... I feel the AIM is due for a decided forward movement. We have been static long enough. (2)*

## MARIE'S ODYSSEY

While Emil and the Marshes were searching out a site for the new Mwanza station, Marie was preparing to return to Africa. Letters to her children reveal the stops along her way:

To Edward from Akron: July 6, 1931: *These next few days will be very busy ones as I leave for the East this coming Friday evening. I expect to be at Keswick Grove from July 11th to 19th. After that my address will be Christ's Home again...*

*I had such a lovely time in Findlay, Marion and Cleveland, Ohio. At Cleveland I had a communion set given me. A pitcher and two cups. Silver, of course. I am so happy about it. I have always wanted a good set instead of just glass bottle and tumblers.*

To Paul from Christ's Home: August 14, 1931: *The Christ's Home Conference begins here the 16th to the 23rd... I expect to be at Westfield for not more than two days while the Westervelt group are there. I will leave for Brooklyn Aug. 25th. We sail the 28th on Friday. I am sorry that I could not get out to Wheaton to see you again but I felt that I could not*

*afford it and I am afraid that you cannot afford to come east
either, especially if you are planning to go to school in the
fall. Naturally I long to see you and Betty again. Seeing Betty
will be out of the question altogether I know. She graduates
the day I sail. I am glad for her sake that there will be this
great event to occupy her thoughts that day instead of having
time to think about mother going to Africa...*

*I have my passport but must get the British visa in New York.
My passport cost $6.00, the visa will cost $10.00 more and the
pictures cost $1.00. Rather expensive business...*

*We have a very wonderful Lord who stands ready to help His
children at all times. Don't forget to get daily help from the
Old Book, "The entrance of Thy word giveth light."*

To Betty and Edward from London: September 8, 1931: *We
reached the Royal Albert Dock some miles out of London
yesterday morning, coming into London by motor buses
arranged for in the boat. Allison's aunt was there to meet me
and saw to my comfort and all those numerous boxes and
trunks, suitcase, steamer chair, etc. ... I bought a helmet
yesterday for 36.00 shillings and mosquito booths for 26.00
shillings. Both are good and I hope to keep in better health
using both... I was surprised to find the Tanganyika Anderson
family here. Mr. and Mrs. and five children... And we are
taking the same boat! Fine, isn't it!*

*As usual London is cold even to frost so I am wearing winter
clothing. And London serves tea for breakfast and I do not like
it for breakfast nor care much for it at afternoon tea, only the
little social part of it. I did have a cup yesterday to warm up.
(3)*

## MARIE REJOINS EMIL

Isabel Severson had traveled with Marie to London. There, the
AIM Anderson family joined them for the rest of the voyage.
When the party disembarked at Dar-Es-Salaam and checked for
mail, Marie was overjoyed to find a telegram from Emil and letters
from many of her co-workers.

From Tanganyika's coast, Marie and Isabel went by rail to Lohumbo. Isabel remained there to continue her work at the Girls' School. Meanwhile, Emil arrived at his old station to meet his wife and take her to their new home in Mwanza; they had been apart for five months. In a letter to Betty, Marie summarized her trip from America:

> It was a long voyage. Let me see, 3,042 miles from New York to England and then 7,029—all together 10,071 miles... I had a welcome telegram from Papa and letters from our Tanganyika Territory missionaries. I expect all of my goods here soon... Miss Severson and I stopped at Lohumbo and Papa met me there. We hired old Kilipo to take our Lohumbo belongings and ourselves to Mwanza. (4)

## COOKING OVER STONES OUT OF DOORS

Mwanza was a scenic town with a lovely waterfront, the second largest city in Tanganyika, and its most important port on Lake Victoria. Large granite outcroppings dominated the surrounding countryside and some even seemed to spring right up out of the lake. Mwanza boasted some city conveniences (a hospital, for example) as well as some urban challenges (such as a prison).

The AIM had a well established church in Mwanza, along with ten outstations, but Emil and Marie would be the agency's first resident missionaries in the city. The grateful Mwanza parishioners pooled their shillings and provided the Sywulkas with temporary housing near the church: two small rooms with a rather wide hall—serving as a third room—between them. Shortly after moving into these cramped quarters, Marie wrote to Betty:

> Father and I are trying to get settled. Pro-tem we have a little 17 x 25 house inside measurements having three rooms... For a kitchen I have a little hut with grass roof which means cooking native fashion. When it doesn't rain I cook over stones out of doors. I do not like the smoke in my face nor the boiled water with the smoky taste...
>
> There is an Arab here that wants to sell a freehold plot for 6000 shillings but there are no mission funds for this. Your

*Father knoweth and Mark 10:29, 30 is still in the Old Book
and the mouth of the Lord hath spoken it. I know that the Lord
has a work for us here and that He will undertake for us. The
harder the problem, the greater glory to our Lord. (5)*

It wasn't until Christmas day that Marie got a real stove. She
wrote excitedly to Paul:

*Dad and I had a quiet Christmas. Services Christmas Eve and
Christmas Day. He took the Victrola up to the Chapel
Christmas Eve. I did not attend on Christmas Day. Stayed
home and cooked the chicken on my new stove which I used
for the first time that day. My! But it is good to have a stove
again after cooking over stones for weeks! (6)*

## HOSPITALITY MINISTRY

Missionaries were constantly coming and going through
Mwanza, for it was not only a busy port city, but also a railroad
terminal. The Sywulka home was always open to friends, no matter
what their religious connection. Marie stretched her kitchen budget
and moved out of her own bedroom when necessary. Snippets
culled from her early Mwanza letters give the picture:

*We have been feasting on mangoes... I have canned some.
With folks dropping in unexpectedly I have to keep a shelf
sacred to sudden hospitality. I have some kraut too in the
making that is to be canned. Tomorrow I hope to make some
jam with pineapple foundation and taste. Don't think I am
spending all my time cooking jams. I am just taking time by
the forelock and making the Lord's shillings go farther too.
When Papa thrusts guests upon me suddenly and without
warning he always says, "Give them what you've got." (7)*

*Papa came back from Ukerewe sooner than he had planned as
word reached us that a Mr. Dahlquist of the Free Swedish
Church of America had arrived at Busia. Papa was to safari
him through the Nzega country to search out a mission
station... So I will be baking another batch of bread etc. Papa
told the folks that he would furnish all the food. In Papa's
mind this means a bit of tea, sugar, bread! As they are going
where there are no stores I am getting extras: potatoes, dried
fruit, beans, tinned goods. Papa will open his eyes when he*

*finds out how much it costs but I feel that I must do this. It is
not at all likely that Mr. Dahlquist would enjoy bugali. (8)*

*This past week, the Nelsons, Jesters and Miss Severson
[stopped here] on their way back to Nassa and last Friday the
Marshes for dinner on their way to Nassa for a little
vacation...*

*Thursday I am expecting three ladies from the American
Lutheran Mission... Don't you think I need a guest house. I
will put two in our bedroom and Miss Samuelson and I will
sleep in the tent. (9)*

*We had company, one German and one Swiss lady from the
Bethel Mission... Nice people and it was a real pleasure to
have them. I was glad that I could speak German, though they
spoke fairly good English...*

*I had four Indian women call on me with six children. One of
the women is a Christian, the others Brahmans—high caste...
How I long to help them and the little children. We are
praying for a native India missionary to work among these
people. There is such dire need. Of course I had tea for them
and although according to their religion they ought not to
touch food with eggs and butter they did enjoy the cake and
cookies. (10)*

## SPIRITUAL CHALLENGES

As 1931 drew to a close, Emil prepared his year-end circular,
trying to summarize the desperate plight of the people around him:
poverty, drought and famine were everywhere, but even more heart
wrenching was the spiritual darkness:

*It is nearly six months since I'm back in Africa, glad to be
back to the great need here. Defeated, deceived, despoiled,
degraded, discouraged souls on every hand. A trip to the AIM
conference in Congo and the affairs of getting a new site in
Mwanza prevented the itinerary ministry I had longed to do
during the dry season... On account of locusts and insufficient
rain the shortage of food is acute and there is little work so it*

*is hard for people to get their tax money of 10 shillings. But
our spiritual need is greatest. Hidden and condoned sin,
headiness, pride, lust, etc. grieve the Holy Spirit. The devil is
ceaselessly bent upon his purpose of deception, persecution
and corruption. God's children are hard pressed and often
perplexed. Our Sunday meetings are good—always some
confessions of sin or of faith in Christ. But so many are
shallow and thorny ground believers. We have both joy and
heartache in our work. Pray for a heaven sent revival. (11)*

## UKEREWE ISLAND

Emil was always on the lookout for possible new stations.
From the Mwanza waterfront, he looked out at Lake Victoria and
thought of Ukerewe, a large, densely populated island with
wonderful orange groves. Roman Catholics and Seventh Day
Adventists had begun small missions there, but there was still
much more to be done. Emil wrote in early 1932:

*In January I visited Ukerewe Island, 40 miles northeast of
here, for the first time. The Roman Catholics have been there
many years. Their converts wear medals of the saints and
crosses. Here and there are some who have been taught in our
mission and by the Seventh Day Adventists. At Ilangala I
found... a nice building made of upright logs and situated at
the edge of a large forest where there are baboons and wild
hogs galore, and where, until last year, the elephants used to
roam and depredate the gardens at night. They were so
destructive that last year, a government official went there and
shot the last ones, twelve in number. But the people still have
to defend their gardens—in the day time from baboons, and in
the night from wild hogs... I stayed there two days and it was
a delight to minister to the little flock of believers who never
had had a visit from a missionary before... Half a dozen
places want schools and teachers. (12)*

Ukerewe presented some unique challenges. It wasn't easy to
find transportation to the island. When Emil managed to get
passage on a boat, he usually took his bicycle along as baggage.
Once on the island, he could then bike from village to village,
often with some little African boy, eager for the ride, on the seat
with him. Once a spill caused severe injuries to both Emil and the

little fellow who was with him, but both recovered. A more serious problem, however, for Emil, was opposition from Ukerewe's chief. Marie wrote:

> *Papa has gone to town to see the chief of Ukerewe about outstations. He is an old heathen and does not favor missions. All the chiefs of the district are to be here in Mwanza this week. This man came over in his own motor boat, if you please. Wish we had one, as much of Papa's work is along the lake stretching many miles. (13)*

## MWANZA SUNDAY SCHOOL ORGANIZED

The Mwanza church had a resident pastor or teacher, a man named Yonazani. But that didn't mean that Emil could take Sunday as a day of rest. Marie reported that he usually preached four times on Sunday! Early in 1932 he also organized a Sunday school for the church. He wrote:

> *Since January we started a Sunday School which includes the whole church. The baptized men and women are all in one class. We take one chapter each Sunday. Began with Matthew and will go right through the New Testament. The others study the catechism and the little ones will begin with the large picture charts... They will meet in our house. We have seven classes now, and teachers and [pupils] seem very interested. I function as superintendent... We begin at 7:15 a.m. sun time. After Sunday School is the church service which is crowded... After the service those who want help are invited to stay for prayer. (14)*

## OUTSCHOOLS

When entering a new area, the AIM usually began by setting up a mission station with a resident missionary in charge. Next, the missionaries visited the local chiefs or other authorities in order to obtain the necessary permission—as well as the needed land—so that they could establish "outschools" or "outstations" in the surrounding villages. These schools were staffed by paid African pastor-teachers who worked under the supervision of the missionaries. These men were expected to evangelize the villages, lead their little flocks in worship, and educate the youth.

When Emil arrived in Mwanza, there were ten outstations already in existence, each with an African teacher in charge. But he was constantly on the road, looking for places where new outschools could be established. His letters give the picture:

> *Last week I went... about 25 miles from here to arrange about a new outschool. We pitched the tent at dark by a tree where cattle hang around at noon time. And for some mysterious reason we didn't make a ditch around. Toward morning a rain came and the inside of the tent was transformed into something like an African cattle pen in the rainy season. Further comment is unnecessary...*

> *I had a very nice piece of land allotted for a school the next day. Came home along railway... Just now I have received permission for 3 schools. Not always easy to obtain. (15)*

> *Applications for four new outschools have been granted. But we need God-given pastors and teachers. A real visitation from God is still our greatest need. We are in danger of being submerged with a lot of detail, little things that press for attention, and real prayer being crowded out. I'm endeavoring to fulfill the promise I made to the Lord in California years ago under the shade of a peach tree—to spend three hours a day with Him. I do not always succeed. (16)*

As the outschool ministry grew, so did the need for continuous training of the teacher-evangelists. Emil rounded them up every month for a whole week of instruction and inspiration.

> *The Sywulkas' concern for a strong church, standing firmly on African feet, focused on the evangelists whom they called together for a week of training in every month. They taught the Bible, sang with them into the night, and, long before the theorists talked about environmental concerns, they expected each evangelist to plant ten trees. (17)*

## CHAPEL CONSTRUCTION

Some brief quotes from the 1932 Sywulka letters show the scope of Emil's Mwanza work: prison ministry, baptisms, preaching, organizing new outschools, and trying to purchase a site where both a new chapel and a missionary residence could be erected.

At first, the prospect looked dim. The Sywulkas were offered a garden property, but while government red tape delayed the transaction, the owners changed their minds and decided not to sell. Emil and Marie refused to give up. By the summer of 1932, they at last obtained some property. Without detailing the trials and disappointments involved in the land purchase, Marie wrote:

> *After much Satanic opposition and severe testing of faith, the present site on Makongolo Road was obtained, a freehold purchased from a friendly Arab. (18)*

Once the site was purchased, Emil found a new responsibility thrust upon his shoulders—this in addition to all his other duties. He was to be in charge of building the new chapel. Marie wrote, rather poignantly, to Edward:

> *Here we are nearing the end of August and it may rain in October. Looks as though we cannot put up our house, but the teacher's, and live in that until we can build a larger house. "Your Father knoweth." I did so hope that we could get settled. I really have not been settled since we left Lohumbo. It is a bit hard on the flesh at my age but we are glad to pay the price if it further His kingdom...*
>
> *Papa has gone off with his Bible for a quiet time. The other day was our 25th anniversary. A very quiet day. Even Papa away. He forgot all about the great day. I missed my family. (19)*
>
> *Your father is over at the [chapel construction] day after day and usually all day long. Seems most days he does not get home for dinner, then he is supposed to take a lunch or send for hot food, a boy coming on a bike. But only too often he refuses to do either and says, "Oh, I'll just have some gruel*

126

*with the folks." I did get him to take a lunch this morning. I'll
have a good hot supper for him tonight...*

*We will not get our house built this season. Both your father
and I want the church to be built first. Much of our house
money is going into the chapel...*

*I know the Lord wants us to have a good house and large
enough for ourselves and others that come and go and when
we get to the building time, He will supply the funds...*

*I want to sell my dispensary supplies... and put that money
aside to furnish a place for guests... Now when folks come in,
we move out. I really do not mind and am glad to do it. (20)*

Emil, working feverishly to try to beat the rainy season
downpours, added his own perspective on the building project:

*The cares of the work press hard and constantly and now the
rains seem to have started earlier than usual and I don't know
if we shall be able to finish our mud brick chapel or not. It
does not look propitious. Perhaps we ought to have built of
stone in the first place but I was afraid of the expense. (21)*

*How I have learned to sympathize with Moses. Getting people
into the promised land is about the biggest job there is this
side of heaven. I've had some joy and a lot of heartache about
this building. These people here are more than willing to let
God and the missionary do it all. (22)*

### "VARMIN" AND AN OLD CAT

Someone once remarked that "the furloughing missionary with
the most lion stories gets the most offerings." In a developed city
like Mwanza, Marie had no "lion stories" to tell, but she had her
own adventures with African wildlife: bugs, spiders, and even her
own cat:

*I had to stop writing to kill a bedbug running across the table.
I'm so glad that I happened to see it. Susana from Magu was
here a bit ago and sat quite close to the table. I suppose she
brought it in with her...*

127

*She is one of the early Girls' Home girls and is doing good work in Magu, especially teaching girls. Papa got home from safari last night so all his safari bedding etc. is out on the line today. These must be looked over for bugs every time. As long as I am writing about varmin, I am reminded of the nasty spider I killed last night. I saw it several nights ago, but it got away from me. It is a venomous looking thing with a body more than an inch long, thick and hairy, long thick legs etc. I asked several people about it and all say it is as bad as a snake and deadly. I saw it first in the bedroom, last night it was sitting near the book box in the sitting room. I put my foot on it in a hurry.*

*The folks had a great time looking at it through my little magnifying glass. Well, there are worse things than bedbugs. Malaria mosquitos for one thing. In the glory time to come when we will have a new earth with its new Africa, then these former things will have no place there. Won't that be fine. And no sin! (23)*

*The old cat has just walked across the ceiling cloth. This is the cat we gave away a month or so ago to a man that lives several miles away from here. When they tried to take her out of the box she up and away and that was the last seen of her. Saturday evening after dark I heard a mewing. I thought, "That sounds as though that cat knew this place and is calling for the cat sleeping on the chair." When I opened the door there stood the old cat—hungry, thirsty, tired and glad to get home at last. (24)*

## CONFERENCE MINISTRY

Early in his Africa days, Emil wrote: "I believe that a missionary should be a person who has learned to endure testings… One must also have a regular habit in feeding his soul daily by communing with God through prayer and study of His Word." A co-worker commented: "That Mr. Sywulka put this advice into practice in his own life is evidenced by the increasing richness of spiritual food that he was enabled to prepare and to set before others." (25)

Missionaries and national workers alike were hungry for the "increasing riches of spiritual food" that Emil set before them in his Victorious Life messages. So his ministry reached far beyond the Mwanza church and its outstations. In 1931 and 1932 he was invited to speak in the Congo, then at the Nera conference, and lastly to a gathering of Lutheran missionaries.

Marie heard plenty of comments about his preaching. At the Nera conference in July, with some 1,000 people attending, Emil preached at the morning service for one hour and 53 minutes! (William Maynard timed him.)

The Lutheran conference was scheduled for October, 1932, when Emil was busiest with the chapel construction. Just in time for the meetings, he purchased a motorcycle which would come in handy for the 130-mile trip. Marie wrote to Edward about the new vehicle and then added:

> *Your father does give messages that meet the need of the hour among missionaries. We still hear about his messages in Congo a year ago. It was the same at Kijabe when we were there on our way to USA. Your father will probably go [to the Lutheran Conference on his] motorcycle. He can make it in a day from Busia providing he keeps going. (26)*

In subsequent years, Emil was invited to speak on the Christian life to gatherings of many different societies. Missionaries from the AIM, the Lutheran Board, the Bethel Mission, the Mennonites, and many others all gave testimony of the impact of his messages on the Victorious Christian Life.

**Emil and Marie with coworkers Dr. Nina Maynard
and Rev. William Maynard**

## *1932 IN REVIEW*

Since Mwanza had a government hospital, Marie decided to sell her "dispensary equipment" to Miss Baker at Kijima. The funds could go toward the new chapel and home. December found the Sywulkas "busy as rabbits in a clover patch" finishing up the inside of the chapel and trying to complete two rooms of a house for themselves. Emil asked Marie to compose the year-end circular:

> *Once a year we have a general conference, usually at our Nera station when our people gather from all over our Tanganyika field for at least four days. I wish that you could see them coming in. A few of the men have bicycles and pedal in, but the great majority have to get there on their two feet, young old, and middle aged, and women with babies strapped to their backs... One old saint walked fifty miles to get to the Conference. No wonder her legs ached. Others came from one hundred miles away. Yes, they walked. There is a lot of greeting and handshaking. It is a joy to meet folks you have not seen for years especially those of "like precious faith." There were some of our girls, formerly of the Girls' Home,*

*now proud mothers of first babies. Of course the babies had to be petted and loved, and of course they crept right into our hearts... Oh these precious African babies, how the tender Shepherd must love them...*

*Sunday was "the great day of the feast." All told there were about one thousand people there, not all believers, for some always come out of curiosity. In the afternoon we celebrated the Lord's supper. A blessed hour indeed. It meant so much to us to receive the sacrament from the outstretched brown hands of men who know what it means to have lived in heathen darkness and who know what it means to have the Light of the world dispel that darkness... Our blessed Lord was in our midst and we felt that regardless of color or race we were "all one in Christ Jesus."*

*...Mr. Sywulka has also had three conferences in our Mwanza district, one over on Ukerewe Island, one at Magu, and another at Busagala. The Magu district conference was one of special blessing. It was here that after a full day of services the evening meeting became a nearly all night service of praise and prayer. This was not man's program but of the Spirit.*

*"Be not forgetful to entertain strangers."... A number of highways center here in Mwanza, while the coast to lake, Tanganyika Railway, has its terminus here. Then there are the Lake Victoria steamers that make regular calls at the Mwanza port. So we have had a goodly number of guests... As we have come in touch with these missionaries of our own board and other mission boards representing various denominations and nationalities may I say once more that we are "all one in Christ Jesus." All are working towards the same goal, winning Africa for the Lord Jesus.*

*We are still living in our wee house so when folks come we usually move out for the time being into the tent. Quite comfortable! When the way opens for the building of our house we hope to have a prophet's chamber or two for God's pilgrims and such as need to come aside awhile and rest. When we mentioned this to a Bishop the other day he said, "That would be a great ministry." (27)*

Marie had spend most of her furlough shuttling back and forth between her relatives. Now, for almost two years, she had lived in cramped quarters in Mwanza. It had been so long since she had felt really settled... so long since could "entertain strangers" without moving into a tent. She would trust God's timing to give her the desire of her heart: a home with room for a prophet's chamber or two.

**References:**

(1)  Letter from Marie to Edward, Aug. 3, 1931
(2)  Letter from Emil to Marie and the children, July 4, 1931
(3)  Letters from Marie to her children, July 6 — Sept. 8, 1931
(4)  Letter from Marie to Betty, Oct. 23, 1931
(5)  *Ibid.*
(6)  Letter from Marie to Paul, Jan. 2, 1932
(7)  Letter from Marie to Edward and Betty, Dec. 31, 1931
(8)  Letter from Marie to Edward, Feb. 22, 1932
(9)  Letter from Marie to Edward and Betty, July 7, 1932
(10) Letter from Marie to Edward, Sept. 20, 1932
(11) Circular from Emil, Dec. 1931
(12) Circular from Emil, April 1932
(13) Letter from Marie to Edward, Feb. 22, 1932
(14) Circular from Emil, April 1932
(15) Letter from Emil to Edward, April 10, 1932
(16) Circular from Emil, April 1932
(17) Anderson, Dick, *We felt like Grasshoppers*, Crossway, 1994, p. 56
(18) Sywulka, Marie, *Workers together with Him*, p. 30
(19) Letter from Marie to Edward, Aug. 19, 1932
(20) Letter from Marie to Edward, Oct. 5, 1932
(21) Letter from Emil to Betty, Oct. 10, 1932
(22) Letter from Emil to Edward, Dec. 4, 1932
(23) Letter from Marie to Betty, June 1, 1932
(24) Letter from Marie to Paul, Oct. 17, 1932
(25) *Inland Africa*, January-February 1945, p. 11
(26) Letter from Marie to Edward, Oct. 5, 1932
(27) Circular from Marie, Nov. 1, 1932

# CHAPTER 12
## Marie's Hospitality Ministry
## 1933 – 1944

*GUESTS AND MORE GUESTS*

While Emil supervised construction, kept up an itinerant conference ministry, and explored unreached territory, Marie coped with endless guests in cramped quarters. She felt strongly that God had called her to sell her dispensary equipment (after all, Mwanza had a government hospital) and take up this new calling in her sixties. Letters to her children reveal the challenges she faced:

*Papa left for Ukerewe Island last Thursday and expects to be gone thirteen days, a long time to be away from the Mwanza work. Pray much that the Lord send the much needed laborers for our Mwanza work and also a house for them. Having folks to look after all the time is a bit hard on me at my age. And some folks can make it very hard--it takes much grace to take them into the family sanctuary especially in overcrowded quarters... I think the Lord wants me to minister to folks that come and go through Mwanza. (1)*

*Papa is in Ukerewe and expects to go on to Musuma—across the island on the mainland. This trip will take him two or three weeks. Mr. Nelson has been here for nine days... Just before he came we had Bishop and Mrs. Chambers here for a week from the Church Missionary Society... I expect a party of German missionaries here in a couple of weeks. (2)*

*Papa got back from the Nera Conference on Thursday evening... My part was praying and supplying food for nineteen people for eight days. I had the vegetables come from Kijabe... the oranges came from Ukerewe and the pineapples from Bukoba. (3)*

*Papa is away on another safari. This time to Buduke where there has been a native district conference. There is to be another at Shinyanga beginning tomorrow I think. The two or three days between these conferences Papa planned to spend at Nzega, the place where the Swedish missionaries finally gained entrance...*

*Meanwhile we here are trying to go on with the building... Won't I be glad when we finally get settled. A lot of our things are still at Lohumbo: books, chairs, dishes, my desk—Papa gave his away. (4)*

*A Catholic padre is in the other room and he and Papa are talking religion... Not a heated argument I am glad to say. This man is a German. How many, many times our German has come in handy. I suppose that I should have made him a cup of coffee—4 o'clock coffee--but I didn't. Made orangeade instead.*

*We have been having quite a lot of company lately. Mr. Maynard, Mr. Marsh and Miss Jorgensen in one bunch. (5)*

*Mr. Stauffer and Papa left for Musuma to look over that field,
as Mr. Stauffer is a tenderfoot and knows no African
languages... I was dead tired after the Chilsons left plus some
CMS folks and... had planned a few days of less strain... when
lo and behold, Pastor Sholton of the Bethel Mission and just
back from Germany appeared on the scene to stay a week. (6)*

Some guests were no trouble to entertain. Others were only
too eager to let Marie run their errands for them. She wrote:

*We do have a lot of business to see to for the folks on the other
stations, especially every other Monday when the mailmen
come in to get mail coming in by the Monday boat and their
coming means more than mail. All AIM mail for Nassa,
Businza and Mwanza goes through our hands. Often there are
parcels to clear, sometimes value them for customs. There are
books... slates, blackboards, pencil clips, whitewash,
medicines and what not to be seen to, gotten in town or
supplied here from our bookshop. I am usually done for at the
end of that Monday, especially if we have guests. However, I
enjoy it and am really glad that we can help our fellow
workers.*

*Some could make it a bit easier if they were more thoughtful.
One woman ordered blue dye. I got dark blue. Not wanted so
sent back. Wanted light blue and none to be had. It meant
extra letters (and stamps) and bookkeeping, all for a few cents
worth of dye. Funny isn't it. Much more might be said. Every
rose has its thorns, "but ain't the roses sweet." (7)*

## AN OLD WOMAN'S SHILLING AND AN INDIAN'S DUCK

Marie's kitchen budget was often strained by the steady
stream of guests, but she also experienced some amazing
provisions. A poor African woman gave a shilling, some Indians
donated poultry, and eventually the guests themselves insisting on
paying a small amount for room and board. Marie's letters tell the
story:

*One of our faithful old women... came and quietly put one
shilling in my hand saying, "You have many strangers." I have
not forgotten that. (8)*

135

*An Indian here was going on a vacation with his wife and had
a big rooster and a duck on his hands. We fell heir to both of
them and it helped solve the food problem for our guests. God
is faithful...*

*I have always had a roof over my head, clothing, and never
had to go hungry because there was no food in the house.
Tested some times to the limit, it seemed, but God was never
too late. "What shall I render unto the Lord?" (9)*

*On the 22nd there were six grown ups and a child came in by
train and left again the next evening by boat. All lovely folks...*

*We certainly had a big washing today, twelve extra sheets,
extra pillow slips, towels, and table linen. One of the lines
came down with the wet clothes so these things had to be done
over. We are all very tired. We have started to make a small
charge because the folks insist on it. (10)*

## THE ROOF IS ON!

By the end of 1933, the Mwanza chapel was completed. Now
Emil and Marie felt they could start work on a missionary
residence. It would include a "prophet's chamber" or guest room,
and the Sywulkas would no longer have to move into a tent every
time guests arrived. Marie wrote to Paul:

*You will be glad to know that the roof is on. We still have the
dining room and bathroom to cement and also the back porch.
I do not know when Dad will get at it. He leaves for Magu—30
miles away, on Thursday or Friday to be gone until Monday.
A new chapel is to be dedicated. (11)*

By the end of 1934, the Sywulkas had moved into their new
house. Marie, thrilled to have the extra space, planned and carried
out some further remodeling:

*I have a guest here, a lady of the CMS and from Australia.
While your father is away I am having part of the back
verandah closed in. I am making a pantry of it. Wish that you
could be here for dinner: soup, chicken pie, creamed
cauliflower, potatoes, salad, pudding, tea. (12)*

Marie, with great care, kept track of visitors, menus and finances. By the end of 1935 the hospitality ministry had lengthened its cords further. She wrote:

> I made some purchases in Nairobi... My table linen, sheets
> and blankets needed replenishing badly and I am glad that
> some extra money came in to me personally with which to do
> this. Having so many guests makes extra demands on my
> supplies. During 1935 we entertained 132 counting babies.
> (13)

## AN UNEXPECTED SHOWER OF GIFTS

Provision for the hospitality ministry began as a trickle with a poor woman's shilling; in time this became a downpour of gifts. Marie received some large checks from concerned friends. Then an unexpected trunk-load of gifts arrived from American Mennonites. With amazement and gratitude, Marie reported in early 1936:

> I received a check too from Miss Jacobson... I need a single
> bed for the prophet's chamber instead of a cot. I expect to buy
> a second hand one for 30 shillings, so Dora's money will go
> for such things... If the Lord spares us I hope that we and
> others will enjoy the comforts of a FINISHED house. It has
> been such a long and hard wait for me...
>
> I had a good dinner for one and all—nine of us, and maybe
> made up the lack to Father and the German ladies of the
> leanness of the past days... I enjoyed having the folks here. All
> left but Mr. Marsh, that evening. Next day Mr. Marsh took the
> nails out of the huge box I found on the back verandah. Sent
> out by friends in Lancaster, Pennsylvania, mostly Mennonites
> formed into a Prayer Band. The box contained a large new
> trunk, and the trunk [contained] all sorts of lovely things—
> clothing from the skin out for me, even a light-weight rain
> coat, so much needed. Father: shirts, socks, three pairs of
> pajamas and so on. My dresses are too large but that is better
> than too small and I can remedy the matter. Then there were
> heaps of all sorts of towels, bed linens and spreads, table
> linens, as three tablecloths and napkins, dresser scarves, all
> kinds of toilet supplies... all sorts of sewing supplies... spoons,
> forks, knives, dried fruit, beans of two kinds, dried corn,
> mason jars, a four-piece flour, sugar, coffee and tea canister

*set, one large Griswold skillet, three cream enamel bowls, and
one large cream and red enamel cooking pot, much too nice to
put on the stove so it is doing duty as a cookie jar. What these
folks did not think of! Not one useless or old thing in the trunk.
I know the getting of things was prayed about and the Spirit
directed. You know these people are strangers to us except
two, some cousins of mine that live in Lancaster. I have said
so many times that we can never get even with God's giving.
What help we gave the Mennonite people in getting started
here in Africa was gladly done as unto Him with no thought of
reward. What the home Mennonites have done for us is a
token of appreciation and thanksgiving to God and us. I do
feel so unworthy of it all. The trunk and contents cost over
$100. Freight, agent, customs, all prepaid. (14)*

## A GUEST HOUSE

As the number of missionary guests burgeoned, Marie and
Emil became increasingly convinced that they needed more than
just a prophet's chamber or guest room; they needed a separate
guest house! Marie later recalled how their prayers were answered:

*One day a letter was received from an old-time friend in
America saying that she was sending us a money gift, no
strings attached! This was the answer to our prayers for the
building of a guest house. Many, many of our own mission and
other societies have found shelter here as various
circumstances brought them to Mwanza to tarry a night or
longer...*

*It gives us pleasure to say to our guests, "Your room is ready;
here is the key; make yourself at home." Our prayer is, "Lord
Jesus, give us the hands of a Martha and the heart of a Mary
for this ministry." (15)*

## WARTIME HOSPITALITY

The stream of guests continued to delight Marie for many
years to come. She always loved children, and "missionary kids"
had a special place in her heart. Eventually, many of them returned
to Africa for careers of their own, and she enjoyed seeing a second
generation of missionaries' children.

World War II impacted missionary work in Africa in several ways. Giving from America dropped, food was rationed abroad as well as at home, and some workers were caught between opposing forces. In 1941, more than a hundred missionaries were sailing to Africa on an Egyptian ship called *the ZamZam*. In spite of the fact that she was neutral, Germans seized the vessel, took the passengers captive, and then sank the ship. The missionaries were eventually rescued.

We quote a couple of Marie's letters from the early 1940's, when she was pushing seventy. They show the scope of the hospitality ministry, which continued growing, unabated even during the war years:

> *We still keep on having missionary guests. My family increases with the years. This year we had two hundred and forty-seven visitors counting grownups and children. Recently in eighteen days we had twenty-nine different folks here: Salvation Army, Church Missionary Society, Bethel Mission, Mennonite Mission and AIM. Even had a guest over Christmas from Uganda and on her way to South Africa... I do want this ministry to be as unto Him and much more than just caring for the physical comforts of those that come and go. (16)*

> *June first we look for a Mr. Sucharan, an Indian evangelist from Kenya... We will cook rice and curry for him and of course brew tea. We too like rice and curry though not as hot with red pepper as the Indian people do. Don't you envy me—having an Indian evangelist in the home? Last week we had a Colonel Siebrits... of the Salvation Army (17)*

All through the war years, Marie kept up a steady correspondence, not only with her far-flung children and her Ohio family, but also with Emil's relatives. The following letter, from early 1942, was written to Emil's only brother, Edward, and his wife Nora:

> *Emil is very weary in body. He needs a several months' vacation somewhere away from the innumerable affairs and at a different altitude and environment. We had our last furlough in 1930. The Lord has been wonderfully good to us and we are very happy to be here. To Him all the praise.*

*My general health is good though a knee has given me a lot of trouble this past year. I still look after the missionaries of our own and other societies as circumstances bring them to Mwanza. Recently two of our missionaries were ill here. Two men of another society missed their boat and had to wait two weeks for the next boat to take them to the other side of the Lake. I am glad that we could take them in. The hotel is expensive and a hotel atmosphere is not a home atmosphere. One of the men had his wife and several children on the ZamZam.*

*Having guests means food, doesn't it. It may interest you to know that all wheat flours—whole wheat and otherwise, have a generous percentage of cornmeal addition. This is legal and a wartime measure. Things turn out surprisingly well, all things considered. Nora, don't you want to run in and try your hand at a sponge cake or angel food with our "Swansdown" flour? I'll stick to butter cake and gingerbread when I feel that we need a cake for company. We out here have good food and plenty of it. I wish we could share with those in want elsewhere. Prices are higher along all lines and some things scarce, things that are imported, especially so. (18)*

For her first two terms in Africa, Marie's calling had been nursing. After moving to Mwanza, she still attended to the cuts and bruises of neighbor children, and did all she could for any ill missionary who was visiting. But in this her third term, in what some might have called "retirement years," she made the guest house her special ministry. Meanwhile, Emil continued his outreach to "the regions beyond." Next, we shall focus on him.

**References:**

(1)   Letter from Marie to Edward, April 4, 1933
(2)   Letter from Marie to Paul, June 1, 1933
(3)   Letter from Marie to Edward, July 14, 1933
(4)   Letter from Marie to Edward, August 2, 1933
(5)   Letter from Marie to Edward, September 1933
(6)   Letter from Marie to Edward, February 1934
(7)   Letter from Marie to Edward, Oct. 19, 1935
(8)   Letter from Marie to Edward, Aug. 11, 1934
(9)   Letter from Marie to Edward, Dec. 11, 1933
(10) Letter from Marie to Paul, Oct. 25, 1933

(11) *Ibid.*
(12) Letter from Marie to Paul, Nov. 1934
(13) Letter from Marie to Paul, Feb. 1936
(14) Letter from Marie to Edward, March 12, 1936
(15) Sywulka, Marie, *Workers Together with Him,* pp. 30, 31
(16) Letter from Marie to Edward, 1941
(17) Letter from Marie to Paul, May 26, 1942
(18) Letter from Marie to Edward and Nora Gray, March 8, 1942

# CHAPTER 13
## 1933 – 1944
## Emil's Literature Ministry

When Emil wasn't on the road, or preaching and praying in Mwanza, he was busy at the translation table or writing tracts. Sywulka letters from the 1930's and 1940's trace his literature ministry.

### KIJITA SCRIPTURES

To his mastery of Slovak, German, and English, Emil had already added four African languages: Swahili, Kikuyu, Shangaan and Sukuma. By 1933 he was learning a fifth African tongue: Kijita, the language of the Majita people on Ukerewe Island.

Marie's letters to her children reveal his efforts to give God's Word to this tribe:

> *Your father speaks Swahili very well and has also added*
> *another African language, Kijita, spoken largely over on*
> *Ukerewe Island... He sure is a* fundi *[expert] at languages,*
> *isn't he. (1)*

> *Papa and the young fellow from Ukerewe have finished the*
> *translation of Luke in Kijita. They stayed on the job day after*
> *day, hour after hour. Now and then when they could not keep*
> *at it another minute they left the desk and exercised at the*
> *wood pile, then went back much refreshed. (2)*

In a 1934 circular, Emil also mentioned the Kijita Luke translation. With typical modesty, he gave most of the credit to his African co-translator Ezekieli Kaneza:

> *The first portion of the Scriptures in the Kijita language has*
> *been translated by a native teacher from the Swahili. It is the*
> *gospel by St. Luke. He and I finished revising it in three weeks,*
> *finished ourselves too. It is arduous work. This, when printed,*
> *will add one more to the over 900 languages in which all or*
> *part of the Bible is printed. (3)*

A 1000-copy edition of Luke in Kijita, translated by Emil and Ezekieli, was printed in early 1934 on the Evangel Press at Lohumbo at a cost of 600 shillings. Marie reported:

> *A Seventh Day Adventist Missionary bought 60 copies as they*
> *have a work among those people (Majita). This is the first and*
> *only literature which the people of this tribe have in their*
> *mother tongue. The entrance of Thy Word giveth light. (4)*

With Luke in print, Emil set his sights on getting the whole New Testament translated for the Majita people. It was hard to find the time for translation, but a motorcycle accident gave him an enforced "rest" period, which he devoted to the project. Marie wrote:

> *I should be out in the kitchen making orange marmalade but*
> *have decided to do it later on in the day... Since I last wrote to*
> *you we attended our yearly Conferences held at Lohumbo this*
> *year. The two Nassa ladies and I went down with the*
> *Stauffers... a 150-mile ride for me from Mwanza. Your father*

143

*decided to go by motorcycle. Near Busia station he had a bad*
*fall in crossing over a wide ditch. The sun shining on a little*
*water made it look like a washout. I do not know if he put the*
*brakes on too suddenly or what. Anyway the fall resulted in a*
*deep ragged tear above the knee... The last day of the African*
*Conference which followed ours, your father began to use his*
*leg and overdid it... so he had to pay for it. He left for*
*Musuma with the Stauffers where he is doing translation work*
*with Mr. Stauffer in the Kijita language. That is a sit-down job*
*so the leg is healing. (5)*

By 1939 Matthew had been translated into Kijita. Eventually
other persons joined Emil, Mr. Stauffer, and the nationals on the
Kijita translation team. These included AIM members Faye Toney,
Frank Manning and Donald Ebeling, along with some Seventh Day
Adventist missionaries.

By 1941, the entire Kijita New Testament was going through a
final check. Emil spent three weeks on Ukerewe proofreading the
typewritten manuscript. Then Frank Manning of the AIM took the
precious pages to New York and personally handed them to the
American Bible Society. Emil, reticent to mention his own part,
wrote:

*The New Testament manuscript in the Kijita language has*
*been taken to the USA by the Mannings for printing. We hope*
*and pray that our people may soon have the Word of Life in*
*their own mother tongue. The translation was first made by*
*the Seventh Day Adventist Mission but later (1941) about five*
*or six months of revision and correction work was done,*
*mostly by Miss Toney and some by Mr. Manning. (6)*

Marie didn't mind mentioning Emil's part in the Kijita New
Testament. She wrote:

*Mr. Sywulka and Miss Toney (AIM) had the larger share of*
*the work of preparing the manuscript for printing. (7)*

Frank Manning stuck by the publication process until the very
end, reading all the galley and page proofs while on his furlough.
The entire Kijita New Testament came off the presses in 1942 and
reached the field in 1943. The first edition was 2500 copies, and a
reprint produced an additional 2000 copies.

The New Testament wasn't Emil's only legacy to the Kijita-speaking people. In 1936, with African helpers, he prepared and printed a Kijita catechism. He also had a hand in the publication of a Kijita hymnal. The believers had limped along with a mere eight hymns until 1936, when Emil printed a songbook with 30 numbers for them. He mentioned the hymnal in a general letter and then added a sentence about the difficulty of producing it. His statement leads us to believe that he himself either wrote, translated, or edited the hymns:

> To write a song to fit the music and to pay attention to meter, rhyme, accent, theology, orderliness of thought etc. is a job, especially when one does not know the language well. (8)

Emil's Kijita hymnal was later revised and expanded with the help of Mennonite missionary Ray Wenger and AIM missionaries Faye Toney and Donald Ebeling.

### KIKEREWE LITERATURE

Soon after printing Luke in Kijita, Emil began dreaming of preparing literature in Kikerewe, the other language spoken on Ukerewe Island. He told Edward that he planned to translate Matthew and also prepare a "first reader" and songs for this people group.

Whether he ever translated Matthew we do not know, but his letters do tell that he produced a hymnal and catechism in Kikerewe. By the close of 1937, these two works, all in one book, were printed and distributed.

### STUDIES IN LUKE

For many years, Emil had longed to produce simple Bible studies for new converts. God had given him insights into Luke's Gospel, and he began to jot down his musings as early as 1911. As the years went by, he continued to refine his notes, and to translate them into both Swahili and Sukuma. He expressed his dream to his son Edward:

> *I have a great longing to put what God has taught me on the*
> *printed page. (9)*

It was hard to find the time to devote to the Luke studies. The press of church and outschool supervision, the many speaking engagements, and the Scripture translation all had priority. But in 1934, Emil spent five weeks as a guest of the Bethel Mission in Bukoba, and there he found time to work on his notes. Marie wrote:

> *Papa has gone to Bukoba. He is all worn out with overwork.*
> *When he says, "I am desperately tired," it means something.*
> *He will probably be gone at least a month. He expects to work*
> *on studies in the Gospel of Luke. It is almost impossible to*
> *keep at a task like that here. Too many other affairs calling for*
> *attention. This will be printed in Swahili and thus be used by*
> *various societies in their mission work. (10)*

> *Your father did not come on yesterday's boat but is staying*
> *two weeks longer. He says that if he comes now he will be*
> *swamped with all sorts of affairs and not be able to finish the*
> *translation work he is doing. He has had this particular bit of*
> *work on his heart for twenty years. The Sywulkas usually do*
> *not give up but keep the goal in view until they reach it. Fine*
> *trait. (11)*

Six and a half years later, Emil was still working on the Luke studies. He wrote to Edward:

> *I ought to have five or six weeks off to finish the questions on*
> *Luke's Gospel begun thirty years ago at Nassa. I think if they*
> *would be printed in English they would meet a wide need*
> *among missionaries. Will try to send you some samples. Am*
> *also working on a tract, "Thou shalt have no other gods before*
> *me." Yesterday I was to a little outschool six miles away from*
> *here. They, like a garden, need attention. God's grace*
> *produces only weeds in uncultivated soil. (12)*

In time, Emil's Luke studies were translated, not only into Swahili, but also into Sukuma. The Sukuma edition was printed in 1943 on the Evangel Press in Lohumbo under the title *Wilanja*. Emil wrote in a circular letter:

*After thirty years "Wilanja" (Self-teacher) —a book of
questions based on Luke's Gospel— has been completed and
printed. It is meeting a real need in Bible study. Several new
tracts have also been produced.*

*Pray for us, that we may be victors in the field of battle. God
reigns from a cross-throne. We also... Prayer is the most
potential of all Christian ministry and also the costliest. Try it
and see. (13)*

## SUKUMA HYMNAL

Marie's *Workers Together With Him* describes the old Sukuma
songbook that the Sywulkas found when they moved to Nassa in
1909. Printed in 1896 by the Religious Tract Society, it was the
work of early Anglican missionaries whose knowledge of the local
language was sadly lacking. Many of the songs contained crossed-
out words and other pen and ink corrections. Two were marked
"very bad," meaning the translation into Sukuma was full of
grammatical and usage errors.

Emil realized the importance of hymnody in worship, and so
from the earliest days he set about to revise the "bad Sukuma" and
to add new songs. Later, Tom Marsh continued revising the
hymnal. In 1928, an edition of 2000 revised songbooks came off
Emil's Evangel Press in Lohumbo.

But Emil wanted an even larger hymnal for the Sukuma
people. In Marie's letters, tucked between mentions of tropical
birds and bread baking, there are references to the songbook Emil
and Tom were preparing:

*There is such a lovely shower that I enjoy watching and then
there is a little wagtail enjoying being out in the rain, taking a
bath and now and then pouring out a volume of song much
like a canary... Now a red bird is calling my attention...*

*Our many mango trees here attract the birds and woe to the
boy that uses a sling shot. We have a lot of mangoes coming
on. They should be ripe soon. When that happens then the
little long tailed parrots will come here to board if not to
room...*

*Last week your father was at Kijima working on the revising
of our Sukuma hymnbook with Mr. Marsh. I expected him
home Friday a.m. and hurried the bread baking as he was
planning to start off again the same day to visit the Magu
outschools. He never got here until Saturday p.m. Said they
had not finished their work. (14)*

Tom Marsh passed away suddenly in 1936, but his work went
on. In 1942, a still larger Sukuma hymnal was printed on the
Evangel Press. And in 1948, an edition of 10,000 copies was
printed by the AIM press in Kijabe.

## SUKUMA NEW TESTAMENT REVISION

The first Sukuma New Testament, translated by Emil, Tom
Marsh, and Lazaro Kihayile, was published in 1925. Later they all
agreed that it needed revision. Emil's 1936 and 1937 letters
mention this project:

*We are now revising the Sukuma N.T. and I find that I know
very little of this language although I have been in this tribe
for sixteen years. And I find that I do not know English well
either. I will be glad if you can tell me the Biblical meaning of
the words "sober," "grave," "godliness," in Timothy. Words
for sin in African languages are not hard to find; words for
goodness are. (15)*

*The revision of the New Testament has been interrupted but
we do hope to finish by next September or October. It is a
difficult and arduous task. (16)*

The Scripture revision, like Emil's Luke studies, took far
longer than he originally anticipated. The Sywulkas had been back
in Africa for a full six-year term, but Emil would not even consider
a furlough until the entire New Testament was revised. Marie
wrote about how doggedly he was pursuing this project:

*Your father is teaching the new missionaries Sukuma, also
working on the revision of the New Testament. He was not so
well when he left: cold, cough and some malaria. I expect him
home this coming Friday for a few days. We are to have all
day services on Saturday and the teachers are expected from
the outstations. That will mean another hard day for your
father and Sunday is always the heaviest day in the whole*

*week. Father is very weary in body and every so often says, "I
would enjoy a two-months ocean trip." I am tired too. Guess
we need a good vacation... Your father says—no furlough
until the revision of the New Testament is finished... Anyway,
there is no furlough money. I said to your father one day, "I
wish that we could save a little towards furlough." He
answered, "No." (17)*

Emil had far too many responsibilities to devote himself
completely to the Sukuma New Testament. In 1939, he turned the
revision project over to Charles Hess, a Wheaton graduate with a
knowledge of the original Greek. Emil then he asked his prayer
partners to remember Mr. Hess:

*Pray for Mr. Hess, upon whom rests the burden of the revision
of the New Testament. It is a very heavy load for one man and
he needs upholding. (18)*

Charles Hess gave himself completely to the task. In 1940, the
manuscript for the completely revised New Testament, in three
installments, reached the British and Foreign Bible Society in
London. But the war was already wreaking havoc in England.
Funds were scarce, and the Bible Society buildings were damaged
by enemy bombs. In 1941, Emil reported:

*The manuscript for the Sukuma New Testament has been in
London since the beginning of 1940, but we have no definite
word that it is being printed. It is seven years since the last
edition was sold out. Surely, the great enemy of God has
defeated us in this. All of us on the field, I think, feel this
keenly. In fact it is deeply painful to us. Our Evangel Press is
endeavoring to supply the need at least in part. (19)*

By 1943 the Kijita New Testaments were arriving from New
York, but there was still no sign of the Sukuma New Testament
from London. Not until 1944, the last year of Emil's life, did it get
to Africa. In all, 12,000 copies reached the field.

### SUKUMA OLD TESTAMENT

The Sukuma Old Testament was at first produced piece-meal.
Genesis was printed at Lohumbo in 1929, with Exodus following
in 1931. Several of the minor prophets came off the press in 1932,

and Leviticus was published in 1934. The rest of the Old
Testament was translated directly from the Swahili by Zaharia
Belele.

Emil was part of an AIM team assigned to revise Zaharia
Belele's work. By 1941, he had sent selected Psalms to Lohumbo
for printing and was working on the Pentateuch. Marie, hampered
by a broken arm and wartime food shortages, still managed to bake
something for his birthday while he was at the translation table.
She wrote:

> Mr. Jester is staying on a few days to help with the Old
> Testament translation work in Sukuma. Your father loves this
> kind of work, but he should be where there are not so many
> interruptions. I think they are working on Numbers. The
> Psalms are at Lohumbo being printed. A separate book...
>
> Today is your father's birthday so we had a special dinner. As
> he likes pie better than cake we usually have a birthday pie
> but not this time. It takes skill to make pie crust with flour that
> is 100% cornmeal... I could not manage with one hand so we
> made pumpkin pie without the crust. In this case, it was sweet
> potato instead of pumpkin. (20)

About the same time, Emil gave his perspective:

> I've sent off the last of some sixty selected Psalms to the press.
> They are now in printing. Am now working on Deuteronomy. I
> ought to have a whole year free to check up on Zaharia
> Balele's translation of the Old Testament. Next week I go to
> Gaita, 85 miles west of here, and other itineraries are due
> soon. I have to guard myself against lethargy in service and
> against lukewarmness toward God and men. (21)

Two years later, Emil and the rest of the team were still
working on the Old Testament revision. Marie wrote to Paul:

> Mr. Ebeling, Daddy and African helpers are still working on
> Genesis. It is a long hard piece of work. Mr. Ebeling has done
> just splendidly at the language and I have great hopes for him
> as to his being our coming language man. Recently we
> entertained for several days a Mr. Guthrie of the African
> Language Dept. (University of London). He is out here making
> a special study of the Bantu language group and especially the
> verb forms... Language was the one and only topic these days.
> I think that if I had given Mr. Guthrie, Mr. Ebeling and your

> *father "wood, hay and stubble" at meal times they would not*
> *have been the wiser, being so absorbed in this one thing. (22)*

Emil didn't live to see the complete revision of the Old Testament. Not until 1961 did the entire Bible in Sukuma come off the press—a 10,000-copy edition. But Marie saw it, and cried tears of joy to hold the precious volume and see her husband's dream come true.

## TRACTS AND ARTICLES

A chapter on the printed page would be incomplete without a brief mention of the tracts and articles Emil produced in Swahili, Sukuma, and English. Tracts mentioned in his letters include "The True Church," "The Carnal Christian," "The Man of Sorrows" and "Man's Efforts at Self Justification".

"The Man of Sorrows" eventually found its way to America and was printed in English by Christ's Home Press in Warminster, Pennsylvania. Another of Emil's very popular tracts was called "Adam, Where Art Thou?" A fellow missionary wrote that it "was the most popular little book that the mission ever printed." He added:

> *The title in the Sukuma language was "Adamu Nli Hali?"... It*
> *is a wonderful and powerful question, "Adam, where are*
> *you?" Dear Brother Sywulka skillfully applied God's question*
> *to Adam in directing the Africans to see their need of Christ.*
> *(23)*

Toward the end of his life, Emil became distressed about some extreme dispensational teaching that he encountered. He felt strongly that all of the Bible was for all believers in every age, and he opposed the notion that certain parables and the book of Revelation were for "tribulation saints" of a future dispensation. He wrote an "Open Letter to a Dispensationalist Brother" and also penned an article called "The War of the Ages." Published posthumously in the *Alliance Weekly*, the article argued that Revelation applies to the believer today. Emil wrote:

> *It has a vital and not a speculative interest for all who would*
> *stand true. To relegate this book to some other age and thus to*

151

*invalidate it to God's tried and perplexed saints is to do them*
*an infinite wrong. Christ's warriors in days gone by fought*
*their battles by this book, and we need it today if ever. (24)*

Earlier in his ministry, Emil had expressed a great longing to put what God had taught him "on the printed page." Certainly not all his fertile ideas got into print. But through the stream of publications that God *did* allow him to produce, that longing was abundantly fulfilled.

### References

(1)  Letter from Marie to Paul, Oct. 31, 1934
(2)  Letter from Marie to Edward, Dec. 11, 1933
(3)  Circular from Emil, Jan. 18, 1934
(4)  Letter from Marie to Edward, Oct. 31, 1934
(5)  Letter from Marie to Paul, July 25, 1936
(6)  Circular from Emil, 1941
(7)  Sywulka, Marie, *Workers together with Him*, p. 38
(8)  Circular from Emil, May 1936
(9)  Letter from Emil to Edward, May 1936
(10) Letter from Marie to Paul, Oct. 31, 1934
(11) Letter from Marie to Paul, Nov. 22, 1934
(12) Letter from Emil to Edward, May 22, 1941
(13) Circular from Emil, Dec. 29, 1943
(14) Letter from Marie to Edward, March 11, 1935
(15) Circular from Emil, May, 1936
(16) Circular from Emil, Feb. 1937
(17) Letter from Marie to Edward, Aug. 10, 1937
(18) Circular from Emil, 1939
(19) Circular from Emil, 1941
        (1)   (20 Letter from Marie to Edward, May 20, 1941
(20) Letter from Emil to Edward, May 22, 1941
(21) Letter from Marie to Paul, May 29, 1943
(22) Letter from Hamilton and Emily Morrow to Judy Shoff, Nov. 26, 1985
(23) *The Alliance Weekly*, Nov. 4, 1953

# CHAPTER 14
# Are We Ready for Revival?
# 1933 – 1944

## CONFERENCE MINISTRY

Letters from the Mwanza days reveal how often Emil was on the road—overseeing outstations, speaking at conferences, even traveling 400 miles to attend a meeting about possible church union. They give us a glimpse of the perils of motorcycle travel, the ever-present danger of theft, and of how little his material possessions mattered to this man of God. Through it all, we see Emil's great longing for revival:

*Here we are plodding along. Yesterday I returned from a native conference 35 miles from here. The last message on "the wrath of God" by a native preacher brought what seemed to be a real breakdown. It is some time since I heard such crying and agony. Some awful sins were confessed, such as we were unaware were being perpetrated in this land. We believe some of the sorrow for sin went deep enough to stir to true repentance. (1)*

*I returned from Dodoma (over 400 miles distant) yesterday where we discussed the possibility of a United Church of East Africa. On my way back I had my suitcase stolen at, or near, Tabora. Glad it wasn't my head or my heart or my faith or my friends or a thousand other things. (2)*

*General gatherings are helpful. Besides the opportunity to hear new preachers, each of the flocks from round about come prepared to recite a portion of Scripture and to sing a new song—one of their own composing. Some of them are very good. At our last meeting they continued reciting Scriptures and singing songs till the early morning hours. (3)*

Emil was called upon at missionary gatherings and "native conferences," not only in Tanganyika, but also in the Congo and Kenya. Lutherans, Mennonites, Anglicans—they were all eager to hear his message. Like other Victorious Life speakers, Emil often drew a parallel between Joshua's conquest of Canaan and the believer's life of trust and obedience. He called upon his listeners to root out the "seven nations" of besetting sins and to "enter in" to a life of spiritual victory.

Marie's guesthouse duties and tight budget usually kept her from accompanying Emil, but she prayed for him and rejoiced in reports of blessing. At the same time, sensing that the Mwanza church work suffered when he was away, she wrote:

> *Your father is a real "regions beyond" missionary and his work takes him away so much of the time. Meanwhile, I am sure the work here suffers. Just at present Paulo is away too for a month at Nera where the teachers are getting a refresher course. The people need to be visited too in their homes. I can no longer do long distance walking. We certainly need more workers here in Mwanza... God is able. (4)*

Emil, too, felt that more workers were desperately needed:

> *With an expanding work we are in great need of trained and tried men. New men are wanting to enter the service of the Lord. We're glad, but sad too, for their very limited knowledge and experience means usually, that they are unequal to carrying on a sustained and progressive work. To feed and to defend the flock of God is serious business. (5)*

> *I have, after nearly 30 years, not regretted my being in Africa. I only wish I had a hundred lives instead of one to invest in eternal values. Much of the seed sown has fallen on unresponsive, emotional, or reoccupied soil, but some has also fallen into good ground and is bearing fruit to His glory. I have nearly 50 schools and churches combined under my charge besides the Mwanza station, translation, itineraries, etc. The harvest is so great and the laborers so few. The multitudes are as sheep without a shepherd and the Lord says, "Give ye them to eat." "Pray ye." "Go ye." It is the compassion of Christ through His people that can meet the world's needs. (6)*

154

### PRISON MINISTRY

The lengthened cords of an expanded ministry provided the Sywulkas with many joys and also a good share of sorrows. In letters to her children, Marie commented on the both the joys and heartaches of the prison ministry:

> *You will be glad to know that Papa's knee is well again. Took nearly three weeks to get well. The first Sunday we put off the baptismal service and the second Sunday we had Isaka, one of our ordained men, come; and he baptized the seventeen folks, five of whom were prisoners. Papa was still unable to walk and did not dare stand up in the water. The services always mean so much to me.*

> *Last week 50 or 75 men were sent here to the Mwanza prison from the Musuma district. Two folks had been killed for witchcraft and the guilty parties in the village could not be found out so the men were all brought here and are in jail for months to come and have to work. These folks never tell on one another unless it is to pay back. I have an idea that nearly all the Kikuyu tribe know who killed Miss Stumpf. So Papa had a large prison crowd Sunday afternoon in the jail. Pray for this part of our work (7)*

Not every prisoner who responded to Emil's invitations was converted, and not all the converts remained true. He described some of the heartaches of the prison ministry:

> *A thing, both funny and sad, happened in the prison yesterday. After the message I gave the invitation for those who wanted to turn to God to come forward. Two Masai (the Masai are a tribe of daring and famous cattle raiders) came forward. I asked them in Swahili if they were prepared to give up raiding cattle. As they didn't understand, a fellow Masai explained it to them in their language. Upon this one of the fellows recanted and returned to where he had sat and the other a few moments later followed suit. This elicited a ripple of laughter from the forty or more fellow prisoners assembled. The two wanted to be religious but were not prepared to give up their pet sins...*

> *The other night a pack of growling, howling laughing hyenas passed right through our yard. The growls were in a deep bass*

*voice and the laughter in a high pitch. It was a spine chilling chorus. The dogs of the neighborhood which had at first barked valiantly were hushed when the hyenas came through. Pity the poor, defenseless sheep. It would be torn to pieces in a few moments by their terrible jaws. The devil and sin are as cruel as that, with this difference—they don't always announce their approach. The "take heeds" in the Bible and the commands to "watch and pray" are many. It is utterly perilous to ignore them.*

*Recently, a man who was in prison two years for murder, was released. He had been the trusted leader of our gospel work for several years. He was mighty in preaching and in prayer. But it was only a little while until he went deep into sin. Some return from the far country but most of them do not. Sin has a hardening effect. God knows what He is about when He permits temptations and persecutions to try the reality and the loyalty of our faith. "In everything give thanks." (8)*

## LONGING FOR REVIVAL

In his letters, Emil often referred to his strong desire for a mighty work of God in the African church. At the same time, he was aware that revival comes at a price. He expressed himself in a 1936 letter:

*The other evening my motorcycle and I made a foolhardy venture to cross a rush of water across a dip-bridge and it nearly turned us into Baptists. I have gotten several soakings recently by rain and mud and water. God grant that we may all get drenched in the Hold Ghost and power. There are tidings of revival from the four corners of the earth. Is God about to do a new thing? Are we ready? Are we willing to pay the price? (9)*

Marie's letters mention some thorny problems in the Mwanza church, along with her own strong desire for renewal among the local believers. The Kijabe church had recently experienced a revival, although it came only after some bitter heartache following the murder of Miss Stumpf. The Sywulkas longed to see a similar work of grace in Tanganyika:

*Since Papa got home from his more than three-week safari he
is trying to catch up with his work. Quite a number of church
problems... One of our three elders has gone off with another
woman. And now word comes that he helped himself to things
out of the book shop and is selling Bibles, other books,
pencils, clips, etc. I do not know how Papa will deal with this
offense of stealing--whether to take it to the government or
not... all this and more causes much heartache. (10)*

*There is Bubonic Plague in town... One of our one-time
Christians is among the dead... It hurt to see him leave the
things of God and in spite of counsel and many prayers...
choose to walk in the way of sin and destruction. Poor boy.
(11)*

*I have never been so conscious of the enemy's working as this
year... Mwanza being a town is a very wicked place... Folks
are here from Uganda, Kenya, Nyasaland and the Rhodesias
and elsewhere. We could take folks into the church by scores
and scores—on their own terms. Well, we have a great
mission field here but alas, not enough labourers... Your
father is away much of the time. Paulo here is a good teacher
but has not much of a shepherd heart...*

*Our greatest need is a good old fashioned revival in our
Tanganyika Territory church... We may have to go through
the fire as they did in Kenya. You will be happy to know that
some of the worst rebels [there] are coming back repentant.
You may recall that the [exodus of members from] the church
at Kijabe and elsewhere too, left but a mere handful in the
church that stood true to their Master. Those were awful days.
Now they will need to build a balcony in the Kijabe church to
take care of the people that are really coming back in verity
and truth. I am so glad for them and for our dear Mr.
Downing who had to suffer the most in those days after Miss
Stumpf's death. They say he is too happy for words...*

*The church cannot hold all that come so the service is held out
of doors... about one thousand people attend... At the time of
Miss Stumpf's death the number went down to just a very
few—from several hundred to about thirty if I remember right.
Those were very dark and discouraging days. The work of
years swept away over night. I am so glad for Mr. Downing*

*who suffered so much at the time but now has the joy of seeing
the enemy defeated. (12)*

## A VISITATION FROM GOD

The following letters, from the last few years of Emil's
ministry, reveal something of his heart longings. We see how
disturbed he was over sin, and how glad he was to see signs of true
repentance. God answered prayer; in 1937 Tanganyika
missionaries and parishioners alike experienced an unusual
working of the Spirit. Emil wrote:

*Since Conference in July, God has been visiting with His
salvation—missionaries and all. For the first time in all the
years our native teachers and preachers have broken down to
where God could bless... How real Isaiah 35 and 61 seem now
and Psalm 126. The cruel, avaricious, unrelenting "old man"
has held sway long enough. "Utter destruction" is the only
remedy for him. I am sure that simply "taking by faith"
ignores the fact that there are seven strong nations to be
destroyed before possession is possible. "Crucified with
Christ" precedes "Christ liveth in me." (13)*

*God has been doing wonderful things here. First some of our
missionaries were delivered from a life of inner struggle and
unbelief and then some of our native brethren got into the
"land of corn and wine." Prayer, confessions, went on all day
and into the night during Conference. Then joy flowed like a
river. Our native brethren were utterly surprised as to what
God can do. Where "sin reigned" now "grace reigns." (14)*

A year later, Emil was still rejoicing in what God had done in
1937. At the same time, he hungered for an even greater work of
the Spirit. He wrote:

*Nearly two years have slipped by since my last printed letter.
The outstanding thing has been the visitation from God
experienced in July, 1937, at our annual gathering. The
blessing of those days is still with us in part. Of course much,
as always, must be sifted by the testings which God allows or
sends. There is a moral necessity for all things being shaken
so that the things which cannot be shaken may remain to
God's glory. Some who maintained an attitude of antagonism*

*toward the missionaries were marvelously changed and set free from inner bondage. Some of us missionaries, too, entered into "that good land." The first Sunday home from conference witnessed a scene of confession of sins without a break way into the night in a number of our village assemblies.*

*In the District under my charge we have felt the effects of it in our local three-day conferences... The last night (Sunday) is usually given over to singing, testimony, and Scripture recitation and it is difficult to stop them by midnight. Most of the several schools have one or two special songs, either native words and tunes made up by themselves, or some of our songs sung in four parts. Some recite whole chapters of Scripture. The altar calls have been fruitful, witnessing many confessions of sin, mainly by believers who have been defeated. Confession of the violation of the seventh commandment is most frequent. But confessions of anger, hatred, theft, disobedience, obstinacy, using snuff, etc. are not wanting. As always, some are set free and others are not. Some confess to pimples while hiding leprosy, and of course are not healed.*

*Quite a few Mohammedans are not only ready but even desirous to listen to the Gospel. It used to be that if any of them ventured to draw near to an open air meeting they would at once be snatched away by their co-religionists. Now they listen undisturbed. Our Bible woman, Rebeka, who was once one of them, has frequent requests from them to tell them the Gospel. Some have become believers.*

*Last January witnessed the first attempt at a kind of synodical meeting in order to bring into being the organization of the African church. Some progress was made but the thing is not so simple as it would appear to be. The chief difficulty is probably the divergent convictions held tenaciously by us missionaries. Even these must have the Cross applied to them. Another meeting is planned for January, 1939. Do not forget to pray for it. The African church cannot forever remain under the patronage of Missions. Unless we leave a well-organized African church here, it will become a prey to wolves in sheep's clothing who will scatter and divide the flock into various and mutually antagonistic sects, each of them headed by a self-appointed and infallible prophet. Already, as a Mission, we have four off-splits to our credit (or discredit) in*

159

*this field. These prophets usually pose as being persecuted unjustly by a Mission that dares to discipline or excommunicate them for their immorality or disregard of all authority...*

*I am rather afraid to say that we have had 99 baptisms so far this year (1938) in this District lest the devil get to hear of it and I will be sorry later... Will you not surround them by prayers? (15)*

In the ensuing years, Emil continued to find that revival fires could blaze brightly, but could just as easily be snuffed out by moral failure and a critical spirit within the church. He wrote:

*Much has happened since I last sent a printed letter. We are witnessing the tragic moral breakdown of a godless civilization and the spiritual impotence of religion devoid of loyalty and Holy Ghost power... I don't think we are as ready for revival as we think we are. When God sends it, then criticism, antagonism, slander... begin to do their destructive work. The flesh, uncrucified, plays traitor with God's power. Only after crossing Jordan could Elisha be safely entrusted with the authority of the heavenly world.*

*Here we are plodding along. The world, the flesh and the devil have not changed, but then, neither has God. He is the great I AM, not the I WAS or the I SHALL BE. The white man's impact on Africa has brought much blessing but it has also brought the curse of new sins. It has greatly wrought for the breakdown of tribal discipline and parental control, and the permanency of marriage...*

*Last January our faithful Mishaka was ordained to the ministry. He gives himself to the work so unsparingly that I have had to admonish him. I've turned over 15 scattered assemblies to his care. He also helps me on my itineraries. I don't see how I'd carry the load without him...*

*In not a few places the believers provide me with private apartments—a nice mud-brick, grass roofed house for my own use. That is much better than lugging a tent along. I have not used a tent in years. I don't need to bother about food either. Everywhere there are a few chickens less when we leave. You ought to taste the chicken and rice that our African women cook. They even give us tea. The poorest teacher will buy a tea set upon the occasion of the pastor's first visit.*

*Among the many problems in Africa, those of marriage are the most perplexing to deal with—problems of dowry, of incompatibility, of unfaithfulness, of childlessness, of polygamy, of partiality to relatives...*

*Mohammedans readily listen to open air preaching. Some turn to the Lord. "The harvest is great, "the laborers are few", "the time is short." (16)*

*The "care of the churches" takes strength and time. There is no easy way to faithfulness except John 12:24, 25—it is a God-ordained way for all eternity. Duties that seem to demand attention constantly threaten my source of supply—busyness is the foe of godliness. All life is full of danger. The only place the Israelites were safe was in Egypt and in the wilderness. There, like a pauper, they had nothing to lose.*

*I have been doing a lot of moving about this year. Next trip is... 80 miles west, to help Mr. Dilworth start operations on a site just recently granted—a parish of about 20,000 scattered peoples.*

*God has visited the Mennonites at Shirate (north of here) in mighty power just recently. We had a visitation in 1937 but much of it was quenched through criticism and much evanesced into mere emotionalism. But the fire isn't wholly gone down. The gate is narrow, the way costly (Phil. 3), the dangers many. (17)*

Emil's very last circular letter shows us his still unfulfilled longing for complete revival, along with his joy at seeing "some here and there" who were "entering into liberty and victory."

*Here we are still plodding on. My wife is "not forgetful to entertain strangers" as they pass through or come for rest or business, and I endeavor to meet the spiritual needs and problems of our African brethren...*

*There is a spirit of lawlessness manifest everywhere—in the home, the church, in the state. Our native pastor here has had to be suspended for refusal to go to another district to which he had been appointed by the Synod... What havoc*

161

*unsanctified affection can make in the work of God. It keeps untold numbers from obeying God's call to service, panders to self exaltation, sunders churches, breeds hatred, and fosters schism... Truly "the carnal mind is enmity against God;" it will defy heaven to please itself. If the believer reserves a part of his personality, however small, for self, that part becomes the devil's workshop...*

*Despite the enemy's raging, some here and there are resisting him, pressing their claims at heaven's throne and entering into liberty and victory. One of the native brethren God is using greatly in ministering the Word. The unction of the Holy Ghost rests upon him and the gift of teaching beyond that of any missionary we have in this field. (18)*

And so, perhaps, at the end of his life Emil was still asking the question he had posed eight years earlier: "Is God about to do a new thing? Are we ready? Are we willing to pay the price?"

**References**

(1)  Letter from Emil to Paul, October 1933
(2)  Letter from Emil to Edward, November13, 1933
(3)  Circular from Emil, January 1934
(4)  Letter from Marie to Edward, June 18, 1935
(5)  Circular from Emil, 1934
(6)  Letter from Emil to Mike Sivulka, February 14, 1935
(7)  Letter from Marie to Edward, September 18, 1933
(8)  Circular from Emil, February 1937
(9)  Circular from Emil, 1936
(10) Letter from Marie to Edward, March 12, 1934
(11) Letter from Marie to Paul, March 28, 1937
(12) Letter from Marie to Paul, March 6, 1938
(13) Letter from Emil to Edward, October 4, 1937
(14) Letter from Emil to Paul, November 22, 1937
(15) Circular from Emil, late 1938 or early 1939
(16) Circular from Emil, October 1940
(17) Letter from Emil to Edward, August 20. 1942
(18) Circular from Emil, December 1943

# CHAPTER 15
## "I Go Aside for my Children"
## 1933 – 1944

### *"FAR, FAR AWAY"*

When Marie returned to Africa in 1931, Paul and Edward were both in college. Betty—living with the McQuilkins in South Carolina—was just about to graduate from high school.

Marie wrote faithfully and systematically to her three children—long, handwritten letters. Even when they didn't write back, her flow of mail to them remained constant. Emil wrote less often but his letters are equally heart-felt.

Edward and Betty tried to write home on a regular basis, despite the pressures of study and work. Paul wrote less often, but there is evidence that he treasured his parents' letters, for he carefully saved them, and in his retirement years he donated them to the Billy Graham Center Archives in Wheaton.

In this chapter, a few paragraphs, culled from much longer letters, give us a brief glimpse into the Sywulka children's lives, as well as into their parents' love, longing, and faith:

### *"I AM LONGING TO HEAR"*

Marie missed her loved ones, especially on holidays and special occasions. But she learned to cope with the separation, committing her children to the Lord's care, even when she had no idea where they were. She wrote to Paul in 1933:

> *I thought of my mother many, many times on Monday her 91st birthday. I wonder if my children thought to write grandmother a letter. I am longing to hear from the three of*

*you... I do so hope that you three can be together again this*
*summer. (1)*

*This is a Christmas greeting from "the old folks at home, far,*
*far away." How our hearts go out to our children at Holiday*
*Season and on birthdays. It would be so nice to have the*
*family together... I am sure the Lord will encourage our*
*hearts in spite of separations. And every loss has gain. (2)*

Marie had always loved children. The local Mwanza
youngsters, coming and going in her home, helped fill a need in
her life when her own family was so far away. She also found
comfort in "going aside" to pray for her children:

*Paul, dear boy of mine... School is just over... so there is*
*plenty of noise made by the houseboy and cook and a little tot.*
*I always like to have a little fellow under foot since I no longer*
*have you and Edward...*

*Before this reaches you Easter will be past. Wish that I could*
*hear some of the good music you have at home. Anyway, I*
*have the Easter joy in my heart. (3)*

*Dearest Paul... I am feeling much better again, am up and*
*about my work but not quite up to par yet. Malaria does*
*weaken one so much and I do not repair as quickly as years*
*ago. While in bed I heard... what I thought was a mighty*
*rushing wind, which turned out to be locusts... I took a look at*
*the one female papai tree... which had several just out of*
*blossom papai on it as big and round as a finger. All gone!*
*Only stems left...*

*I go aside to pray for my children that the Lord who "waits to*
*be gracious" will meet your needs for body, soul, and spirit.*
*(4)*

Some years, Emil and Marie received only a signed Christmas
card from Paul. They were not, however, altogether without news
of his doings; Edward forwarded the letters Paul sent to him, and
Wheaton friends supplied Emil and Marie with second-hand
updates. Yet Paul's parents felt bewildered by his seeming
indifference, and prayed even more for him. Marie wrote to
Edward in October 1934:

*Thank you so much for Paul's letter. We have not heard since
Christmas. Papa says that maybe Paul resented something
that Papa wrote to him. I'm sure I don't know what it could
have been. In a picture of the graduating group in the
Wheaton College Bulletin there is a person that I say is Paul.
Papa thought so too. I hope we are right... We must continue
to stand by him in much and prevailing prayer, with
thanksgiving. (5)*

Christmas of 1934 came and went, and still Emil and Marie
had no letter from Paul. Marie wrote to Edward:

*I missed my family during the holidays... No word now from
Paul for a bit over a year. If I looked at circumstances I would
be utterly discouraged but my eyes are upon God and I know
that He will not fail. (6)*

## BETTY'S TRAINING

While Paul was in Wheaton, Edward was either studying in
South Carolina or traveling with the Westervelts. Meanwhile,
Betty worked at the Keswick, New Jersey, summer conferences,
then continued her schooling in the fall. Marie wrote to her:

*How fine it is to have a daughter of my own. So many folks
cannot say that. I find myself thanking my Father so many
times for Papa and my three children. (7)*

*My own dear Betty, I think this is your first day at Keswick...
Mother has been praying much for you and the rest of the
young folks who are there to help with the work. First days are
nearly always hard days but as thy day so shall thy strength
be...*

*Since I last wrote to you I have been ill. Nine days in fact and
no wanting of food. It left me as weak as an old rag. It would
have been so nice to have had you here, my dear. My help was
a half trained boy. He can make a cup of tea, and that is, or
rather was, a help. Papa was on safari as usual. Anyway I did
not have to worry about getting food cooked for him. Every
cloud has its silver lining.*

*Wish I could have seen your paper on Alexander McKay. Had
I known in time I would have given you a few facts not found*

*in books. I still have his table at Lohumbo and plan to have it brought here when we have room for it. (8)*

*You really should not accept so much committee work since you have had to help yourself so much by working your way through school. Let the folks do it that have only their studies to look after.*

*I'm afraid that my long distance advice has not done much good. In your studies you are doing the best you can, I know. Yes, health is more important than cramming for an education and overdoing in order to get good marks. (9)*

Emil and Marie never attended a single commencement of their children. Marie was on the high seas when Betty graduated from high school. Two years later, when Betty finished her Bible course, they were still apart. Marie wrote to Edward:

*I wonder where this will find you and where Betty is for the summer... Sorry that I cannot help Betty out with the $100.00 entrance fee to the Philadelphia General Hospital... The Lord may have some other place for Betty. (10)*

*I am wondering if Paul got to Columbia for commencement. I doubt if he could afford it. I shall be waiting to hear all about commencement and then about Betty's plans for the summer and fall... If it is God's plan for Betty to have hospital training then He will make it possible. (11)*

**Betty in her college days**

The Lord *did* make it possible for Betty to have hospital training, even without financial help from her parents. She followed Marie's footsteps, completing a very demanding course at the Philadelphia General Hospital. Often she was so exhausted at the end of a hard day that she could hardly hold her head up, but she still managed to compose regular letters to her parents. Then came the happy graduation day. Marie wrote to Paul:

> *The last mail brought us an invitation to attend Betty's Commencement. I am so glad that she is taking a full course instead of just a year of practical nursing... I am so sorry that I have not been able to attend any commencement of which my children have been a part. My part has been to pray that this goal be reached and now I rejoice in answered prayer. (12)*

### EDWARD'S MISSIONARY CALL

In 1932, Edward graduated from Columbia Bible College. Through the ministry of L. L. Legters, he felt called to serve among the indigenous people of Latin America. When Marie learned of his plans, she wrote:

> *So you have decided that it is not Africa for you... Somehow we had just sort of taken it for granted that it would be Africa for our children, but the Lord knows our hearts. We want you in the place of God's choice for you and not our choice.*
>
> *Before you were born you children were put on the altar and we have never taken back the gift. In the words of Hannah I can say, "For this child I prayed, and the Lord hath given me my petition which I asked of Him. Therefore also I have lent him to the Lord. As long as he liveth he shall be lent to the Lord for service in the place of the Lord's appointing."*
>
> *I'll still be bringing my "little coat" to the temple for you, the garment of prayer and praise. Guess missionary mothers are made that way.*
>
> *Wonder what Board are you thinking of going out under and is it Central or South America? (13)*

Emil, too, wrote to his son. His letters reveal something of his own longings, his views about material possessions, and the type of advice he would give to a young missionary:

> *Your facing toward Central America we leave in the Lord's hands. Probably the fields nearby are as needy as those farther away. I trust you'll not be disappointed with the Mission or with the field. I had hoped you'd go to poor Portuguese East Africa. If the way should open I'd still go. The Lord's will be done. Just so we don't mistake our emotions for His leading. Some do. God abundantly compensates every renunciation for His sake. He did Abraham. He gives good wages...*
>
> *About changing your name—we leave that with you. Feel free about it. Some of our relatives spell theirs Sivulka which looks much easier... Will not change ours—it has served its purpose thus far. (14)*
>
> *Probably this will reach you in Guatemala... I'm glad you're on the firing line. I had hoped it would be Portuguese East Africa. The reasons for our unsolved wishes will be plain some day. I am hoping God will permit me to go there some day.*

*When the Lord said "every creature" He thought of
Portuguese East Africa too.*

*I trust you did not load yourself down with too much stuff (Mt.
10). That has greatly hindered missionary extension in the
past. Surfeiting isn't limited to eating. I find a spare meal is a
great asset to prayer. I hope some time to write on Gal. 2:20
and other theological matters.*

*I am glad you've run the race well thus far and I trust you'll
continue till the prize is won. With true love, Faithfully your
father. (15)*

## EDWARD'S ENGAGEMENT

After three years as a single missionary in Guatemala, Edward
announced his engagement to Pauline Burgess, daughter of
Presbyterian pioneers in that field. Emil expressed his delight:

*Needless to say your last short letter announcing your
engagement called forth love, joy, and praise to God. I am
happy over it and the Lord bless you and Pauline in this new
relationship, enrich your lives and bless the world you live in.
I have confidence, of course, that neither of you will make the
other a rival god. How delighted God must be with an
absolutely undivided loyalty such as Abraham's. We can only
keep what we give...*

*Well, Pauline, know that we welcome you to our hearts and to
that fellowship in our Lord that wonderfully sanctifies all
human relationships. We want them all to be sanctified and
glorified in the cross, blessed cross. (16)*

## BETTY'S RETURN TO AFRICA

In late 1937, while Edward and Pauline were making wedding
plans, Betty was preparing to sail back to Africa as a bona fide
member of the AIM. Emil and Marie had hoped that at least one of
their sons would return to Africa as a missionary; instead, it was
their daughter who fulfilled this dream. Marie wrote to Edward:

*It will indeed seem strange not to write to Betty in America. No doubt she left New York Nov. 1st as planned. I do hope to send letters to the various African ports beginning at Cape Town... I am sorry that you could not see each other again. Betty's heart is certainly knit to yours. (17)*

Betty's coming brought much comfort to both her parents. Marie needed a good rest; and with Betty to care for Emil and the constant guests, she felt free to get away for a week. She wrote to Edward:

*I am at our Businza station where the Jesters live, about twenty miles from home by water. I enjoyed the motorboat ride over here and since coming here I have just been plumb lazy. I have been very tired for some time but it was hard to get away from home. I hope to return tomorrow having been here a week. It has certainly been a comfort to know that Betty is caring for her father's well being. The cook has been off a month sick, and the new houseboy does not know much. It is so quiet and restful here...*

*I have a special interest in some of the boys here. I call them my babies, having welcomed them into the world or held them in my arms when they were just little things. I trust that this school will mean much precious fruitage and a real factor in the furtherance of the Gospel through these boys as they grow into manhood.*

*Our Girls' School is at Lohumbo. I think there are some sixty girls there now. Of course we still have our regular main station and outstation schools.*

*Since Miss Toney was transferred to Ukerewe Island we are minus a good teacher. So our own school does not amount to much not having a trained African teacher either. Father teaches Betty [the Sukuma language]. This father-daughter class makes quite a pleasing picture. Betty is doing quite well at the language. (18)*

## EDWARD'S MARRIAGE

Edward and Pauline were married in high style on February 5, 1938. The wedding, attended by missionaries and nationals from all over Guatemala, was held in Bethel Church in Quezaltenango. One guest is said to have come merely out of curiosity to see the "African" whom Pauline was marrying.

**February 5, 1938 – Quezaltenango**

Marie and Emil had not been able to attend any of their children's commencements; now it appeared they would not attend their children's weddings. But Marie did not complain. Her letter to the newlyweds reveals only feelings of joy:

> *Our dearest loved ones Edward and Pauline: I cannot begin to tell you how happy we are for you and with you. And we certainly appreciated the cable. That was unexpected. I feel greatly enriched in having another lovely daughter. The Lord is good and to Him all the praise. The Lord shower his blessing upon you and grant you many years of united service for Him.*
>
> *And isn't it great to have Betty here. Only I cannot get quite used to her grown-upness along all lines.*

171

*Father has gone to Nassa and I am writing this in bed.*
*Decided to come down with malaria. Dr. Blakeslee was right*
*when she said, "It's from the pit."*

*I imagine there will be some wedding pictures coming this*
*way. We want to send a little gift through Brooklyn but I will*
*not be writing for a few days. (19)*

By the close of 1938, Betty had been transferred to the Kola
Ndoto (Busia) station where her nursing skills more needed than in
Mwanza. Here Dr. Nina Maynard, who ran a makeshift clinic
under a tamarind tree during the difficult days of World War I, had
developed a fine hospital with medical, surgical, and maternity
wards. Marie wrote to the newlyweds:

*You really should have a letter from home to wish you a*
*blessed Christmas and a very happy New Year. I trust that this*
*will reach you in good time. This will be your first Christmas*
*as Mr. and Mrs. Sywulka. The Lord grant that it may be but*
*the first of many more down the future years if He tarry.*

*I am sorry that the members of our family cannot be together.*
*Betty wants us to come to Busia but I am rather doubtful if we*
*can get away...*

*I still see to the comfort of the folks that find their way to our*
*home. Miss Baker and Miss Norton came in just as we had*
*finished dinner on Tuesday. I had hardly finished saying that I*
*was not expecting guests for some days and, "We always put*
*an extra potato in the pot for the unexpected guest" when they*
*appeared on the scene... I am glad for this ministry and I want*
*it to be as unto Him. (20)*

## PAUL'S MARRIAGE

Paul Sywulka was married November 3, 1938—just nine
months after his brother Edward. His bride was Nance Dixon, a
preacher's daughter and a teacher of French at Wheaton College.
When Marie learned of the marriage, she wrote to Edward:

*I too am glad that Paul is married. We had no word from him*
*for more than a year and a half, so did not know that he was*

*engaged. We have heard from several sources that she is a*
*very fine girl. "A fine Christian." (21)*

## FIRST GRANDCHILD

Anna Marie Sywulka made her appearance in February 1939, up in the cold, high mountains of Guatemala. As soon as Marie got the news, she wrote:

> *Our dear Edward and Pauline: How very glad we were to*
> *hear from the two of you and how we rejoice with you. I am*
> *certain that you are proud parents and rightfully so. As for we*
> *two out here, well it seems most too good to be true. We thank*
> *the Lord for the honor He has bestowed upon us. "Great is*
> *His faithfulness." And to Him all the praise. Ever since we*
> *heard that baby was on the way we have been praying for you*
> *in a special way. The little lady sort of upset your well laid*
> *plans didn't she, and came when she pleased. I am so glad*
> *that there was doctor and a nurse. I am wondering if the baby*
> *will have curly hair. If so it will be a fourth generation trait*
> *beginning with my father and maybe before that for all I know.*
> *I imagine Betty will be so excited that she will get off an*
> *airmail letter to you. I sent the letter off to her the same day*
> *we received it.*
>
> *Edward, I am sure that your grandmother Sywulka will be*
> *pleased to know that there is another Anna Sywulka in the*
> *family. Aunt Anna Baumert too. And of course we here.*
> *Thanks very much for adding the Marie too. I will try to be*
> *worthy of the honor and all the more so since my little*
> *granddaughter has both my names though I do not use the*
> *Anna very often. (22)*

## BETTY'S ENGAGEMENT

Betty was not far behind her brothers in finding a life partner. The man God brought into her life was Stephen Jones Barrett. Raised in Missouri, he had become a missionary to South Africa, where he joined an aunt and uncle in serving the Lord. Marie, who saw the entire romance take place right under her nose, described it to Paul and Nance in late 1939:

*This is no surprise to us since coming events cast their shadows before them but it will be a surprise to you and all the rest of our kith and kin. Stephen and Betty knew each other in Columbia Bible College but had no interest whatsoever in each other. However, since coming to Africa there has been letter writing between them which eventually took the color of more than mere friendship. Finally Stephen decided to spend his vacation in Tanganyika—Tanganyika meant Mwanza! He reached here Sept. 10th and left again on the 26th. Between those dates they could talk face to face concerning the affairs of the heart with the result that they are engaged. They are indeed very happy. So are we, for Stephen is a splendid young man. I have fallen in love with him myself and he has a big corner all his own in my heart. (23)*

Stephen and Betty planned to be married in South Africa. But they had to postpone the wedding until Betty could get a proper visa and passage. Marie wrote to Edward and Pauline:

*Betty is still with us. It took a long time to get entrance papers to South Africa and to hear from the government. Now it is a matter of getting passage on East Coast boats. Things are difficult but we know that nothing is too hard for God and that He will perfect that which He has begun. This delay is a bit hard on Stephen and Betty.*

*Your father returned last Wednesday after being away about two weeks. He was speaker at the Missionaries' Conference of the American Lutheran Mission here in Tanganyika...*

*Let us know what our Anna Marie says and does... How I long to see the little family in Guatemala. When? We have no idea.*

*Folks are sweeping and dusting in the church, getting things in order for tomorrow's services. I will do my part in preparing for Holy Communion. (24)*

## BETTY'S MARRIAGE

Despite tight finances and wartime restrictions, Betty eventually got to South Africa, where she would join her husband in his work among the Zulu people, under the South Africa General Mission.

Marie must have felt doubly wistful. Betty was her only daughter, and this was the family's only Africa wedding, yet she was unable to attend the ceremony. She wrote to Edward and Pauline in 1940:

> *As you probably know, Betty was married July 12th... I am sorry that we could not be there, but Miss Slater was on a vacation in Durban and helped with the preparations and represented us and the AIM. It meant so much to me to have so old a friend there. (25)*

From Durban, Mary Slater reported to Emil and Marie:

> *It was a great privilege to be here at Betty's wedding. I was thinking of you all the time. Everything went off lovely... The room looked lovely with greens and roses and other flowers...*

*The audience, about fifty, standing sang "Majestic sweetness*
*sits enthroned," three verses. Then Mr. Hervey went through*
*the ceremony which made them man and wife. (26)*

Mr. Hervey added further details to the letter, describing
Betty's lovely white gown and long train, and mentioning that she
had made her own three-tier wedding cake for the occasion.
Marie shared her feelings with Emil's brother Edward:

*Have you heard from Betty? We miss her, but her happiness is*
*our happiness. Stephen is a fine young man. She is hundreds*
*of miles way from us. Of course she must learn a new*
*language, and Zulu with its clicks is not easy. Pray for her.*
*(27)*

## MORE GRANDCHILDREN

Paul Emil was born to Edward and Pauline on May 4, 1940,
but Emil and Marie didn't learn about his birth until July, after
Betty's wedding. Marie wrote:

*Precious Edward, Pauline and babies: Your airmail letter*
*telling us of the coming of our little grandson finally reached*
*us after being on the way nine weeks. Some of our American*
*letters recently were on the way three months. I try to*
*remember that David Livingstone's letters were two years old*
*when they reached him in the heart of Africa. Well, we are*
*happy, thankful, more than pleased and elated. How rich we*
*feel—two grandchildren! Praise God from whom all blessings*
*flow. (28)*

Emil added his congratulations and expressed his heart's
desires:

*I have time only for congratulations to you upon the arrival of*
*Paul Emil. I pray that he be a Paul indeed who will contend*
*for the faith once delivered to the saints and, of course, live it*
*too. We rejoice with you in this your new and added joy. May*
*he be loved with a Calvary love and not be a rival of the*
*Cross.*

*Here the constant pressure of work and is itself a rival to the*
*prayer time I long for. A parish of 100, 000 is a big load.*
*There are outside calls, too. To possess our possessions is*

*difficult, to keep them even more so. To fight and keep the soul
sensitive is not easy. (29)*

A third grandchild, Paul Andrew, was born in Illinois in April
1941. Emil expressed his joy to the happy parents, and added some
admonitions and a tract:

> *Dear Paul and Nance... Heartfelt congratulations to you on
> the safe arrival of a new Sywulka addition and gratitude to
> our God for the gift of new life. All the possibilities of sin and
> of holiness, of sorrow and of joy, are before it. Yours is an
> abundant joy, also a divine responsibility. The impress of your
> life is found to stamp itself on your offspring whatever your
> creed. Here we are living in difficult days; a hardness is
> settling down upon the church and, of course, upon the world.
> The materialistic, hedonistic days of Noah's day are actually
> upon us. But God is still on the throne. The enclosed is vital.
> With love, your father, E. Sywulka (30)*

As Christmas of 1941 approached, Marie couldn't help
thinking about the grandchildren whom she had never seen. Nor
could she help reminiscing about her own days as a young mother.
She wrote to Paul and Nance:

> *The Lord grant you a blessed Christmastide. This year you
> have the little fellow. That will make all the difference in the
> world. How well I remember your first Christmas in the family
> circle and the Christmas party when some forty of our school
> boys living on the station received their gifts of shirt and loin
> cloth etc. all seated on the floor. You sat on my lap, Paul, and
> you kept reaching out in all directions, not for the gifts but the
> wooly pates of the boys at our feet. It was great fun for them.
> (31)*

To Edward and Pauline, about to begin their first furlough, she
wrote:

> *I wonder where Christmas will find you and just how the
> babies will accept it. I trust that the family will have as lovely
> a Christmas as we did on our first furlough home with our
> babies... Here or there, praise God we have a message of
> good tidings of great joy. (32)*

Marie's letters to Betty and Stephen aren't available, but they
probably expressed similar thoughts, for the Barretts were also

celebrating their first Christmas as parents. Little Grace Marie had joined their home in South Africa on May 21, 1941.

In 1942, a second daughter was born to the Barretts—the fifth grandchild for the Sywulkas! Marie wrote to her son Paul:

> We had the following telegram: "Elizabeth Ann born May 18th. All well. Barrett." I am glad that is over with. Though I do think Elizabeth Ann might have waited until the 20th, your father's birthday, or until the 21st, her sister's birthday, even if she was in a hurry. Betty has had a lot of malaria and because of this and the baby coming, the Executive had her go to one of their stations in Swaziland. Baby was not expected until middle of June...
>
> Betty will have her hands full with two babies. I long to help her. (33)

Betty wasn't the only one who had her hands full! By November 1942, Ed and Pauline had a third baby: Stephen Robb, and a year later Paul and Nance's family was complete with the birth of a second son: Richard Anthony. Because of war conditions, Paul's letter telling about the new baby took six months to reach Emil and Marie.

Richard's birth brought the Sywulka grandchildren to a total of seven. Emil and Marie hadn't seen any of the tiny tots, much less rocked or kissed them. Pictures—snapped and developed at some sacrifice during the war years—helped fill the gap. Marie wrote to Edward and Pauline:

> We have the airmail letter [which] contained the snapshot of Anna and Paul. My! How the children are growing. And how pleased we are to have the picture. We are still waiting for wee Stephen's picture...
>
> We had our missionary conference at the Nassa station in July... I have not been to Nassa for some years. When I do go, I always see things as they were when we lived here, most of all you children when you were little... We used to go out and watch the sun set—a huge ball of fire, or as the people say, "fall into the lake." I did so again one evening and though I missed the loved ones, my heart was so full of praise to our gracious Lord for all the way He has led all down the years. (34)

## WORLD WAR II'S IMPACT

Even while new babies were joining the Sywulka clan, young men were falling on the battlefields of Europe. As the fighting escalated, three of Marie's nephews—Milo, Johnny and Donald—joined the service, and eventually her son Paul was deployed overseas. Marie's letters reveal her concerns:

> *Now and then we have military men visit us when passing through Mwanza. Men who are hungry for Christian fellowship... We had three chaps here one day and Mr. Harper, a CMS missionary and chaplain in the forces, went away so happy because he had his arm full of good reading matter, magazines like the* Evangelical Christian, *etc. Recently word came that he was missing and now that he is dead. We all feel it keenly... I wonder how Milo is getting along and Donald Mason. Donald is so young. (35)*

## LOSS OF BOTH MOTHERS

The war years brought personal losses as well to the Sywulkas. Marie lost her mother in 1938. Elizabeth Wiegand Schneider had lived a long and sprightly life, buoyant to the end. But now she was gone. Paul wrote to his brother Edward: "I am sorry for Mother's sake that they did not come home on their furlough when it was due, so that she could have seen Grandmother before she died." (36)

**Elizabeth Wiegand Schneider**

In early 1940, Emil lost his mother. Anna Jaromisz Sywulka had borne ten children, buried four, and worked long hours to support the six who lived. Marie wrote to Edward. "I suppose that you had word that Grandmother Sywulka has gone home. I am glad that she is at rest. (37)

### BETTY'S ILLNESS

The loss of both mothers, the war news, and the Mwanza church conflicts were sorrow enough. But an even greater shadow was falling across the Sywulka family; Emil and Marie learned that Betty had developed tuberculosis. More than ever, Marie felt impelled to "go aside for her children." She wrote to Edward in October 1943:

> *I always send your letters on to Betty. I wish that you could write to her now and then. Your only sister, Edward. We have two recent letters from the Barretts. The first of three did not reach us though sent airmail. The family were on a much needed holiday in Pretoria. They enjoyed the change of scene and climate and the fellowship with God's people. Betty has*

*not been very well. She had a go of "flu" in July and has had trouble with a bit of pleurisy and a slight cough. In spite of their good vacation she just could not throw off the utter weariness of body. She has been under the doctor's care. He decided on an X-ray of the chest which revealed that both lungs were in the beginning stage of T.B. infection. This came to them as a terrible shock...*

*Betty has been ordered to take six months of absolute rest. She will go to a Hospital in Durban for treatment... The Lord has given them blessed peace, rest, and heart quietness and there is a real note of victory in their last letter. Though our hearts are sad because of their sore trial, we too have peace and rest and quietness. I firmly believe that the Lord will heal Betty and meet their every need. I think a friend will care for the babies. (38)*

In a letter to Edward, Emil mentioned his concern for Betty as well as for his field:

*There are many leakages of power and weights that impede progress—friends, cares of this life, fleshly ambitions, lethargy, an undisciplined life, etc. The biggest leakage is via the tongue.*

*I am plodding on but not accomplishing much these days—not feeling too well. Then, too, there is much opposition here in my section especially Mwanza... There is a threat of starting a new church. In South Africa there are over 600 schismatic churches. I wonder if this is peculiar to Africa. Our loosely organized and governed "faith missions" suffer most from this evil—the spirit of anarchy. The world has affected Africa greatly. Well, even strife and turmoil and upheaval is better than Laodicean complacency.*

*The news regarding Betty cast a shadow of sadness on us but we know the sun is still shining and God is not upset. He has His purposes...*

*Perhaps I better include the English of my new tract, "Marks of the New Birth", in this letter. It is partly from Bishop Ryle's article and partly mine. It is not copyrighted.*

*Have you considered the subject of the baptism with the Holy Ghost? I read Acts 19 again this morning. Here is the church's secret of powerlessness. But I know the price is too high. (39)*

As 1944 came to a close, Emil's responsibilities were heavier than ever. He had not had a furlough in thirteen years, and the pressure of an ever-growing parish with all its blessings and problems weighed heavily upon him. Despite extreme weariness, he sat down to write a Christmas greeting to Paul and Nance:

*Christmas is still a good ways off but by the time this reaches you it will be around Christmas time. So may I wish you and yours a very blessed Christmas and also a God-blessed New Year! It will not fail to be so if you are in accord with the will of God. Harmony with Him spells life and disharmony spells death. It is highest reason to be at one with Him. This means, on the negative side, the removal of everything that grieves or quenches the Spirit of God—often times a very painful operation but, oh, how blessed to be healed. We are well and busy every day. Trial and testing and service are the chariots of God that make glorious riding. But for many they are a juggernaut. May the reincarnation of Christ, in terms of human life here on earth, be a glorious reality to you. Faithfully, your father, E. Sywulka (40)*

Emil could not have known that those lines would be his last to them.

**References:**

(1) Letter from Marie to Paul, July 21, 1933
(2) Letter from Marie to Paul, Nov. 12, 1933
(3) Letter from Marie to Paul, March 12, 1934
(4) Letter from Marie to Paul, June 14, 1934
(5) Letter from Marie to Edward, Oct. 8, 1934
(6) Letter from Marie to Edward, Jan. 4, 1935
(7) Letter from Marie to Betty, July 1, 1932
(8) Letter from Marie to Betty, July 17, 1932
(9) Letter from Marie to Betty, March 24, 1933
(10) Letter from Marie to Edward, May 30, 1933
(11) Letter from Marie to Edward, July 14, 1933
(12) Letter from Marie to Paul, July 1936
(13) Letter from Marie to Edward, Aug. 19, 1932
(14) Letter from Emil to Edward, Dec. 4, 1932
(15) Letter from Emil to Edward, July 19, 1933
(16) Letter from Emil to Edward, Oct. 4, 1937

(17) Letter from Marie to Edward, Nov. 4, 1937
(18) Letter from Marie to Edward and Pauline, March 29, 1938
(19) Letter from Marie to Edward and Pauline, Feb. 10, 1938
(20) Letter from Marie to Edward and Pauline, Nov. 17, 1938
(21) Letter from Marie to Edward and Pauline, March 15, 1939
(22) *Ibid.*
(23) Letter from Marie to Paul and Nance, Oct. 5, 1939
(24) Letter from Marie to Edward and Pauline, June 1, 1940
(25) Letter from Marie to Edward and Pauline, Aug. 2, 1940
(26) Letter from Mary Slater to Emil and Marie, July 1940
(27) Letter from Marie to Edward and Nora Gray, Oct. 14, 1940
(28) Letter from Marie to Edward and Pauline, Aug. 2, 1940
(29) Letter from Emil to Edward and Pauline, Aug. 12, 1940
(30) Letter from Emil to Paul and Nance, July 28, 1941
(31) Letter from Marie to Paul and Nance, October 1941
(32) Letter from Marie to Edward and Pauline, Oct. 20, 1941
(33) Letter from Marie to Paul and Nance, May 26, 1942
(34) Letter from Marie to Edward and Pauline, Sept. 3, 1943
(35) *Ibid.*
(36) Letter from Paul to Edward, Nov. 28, 1938
(37) Letter from Marie to Edward and Pauline, June 1, 1940
(38) Letter from Marie to Edward and Pauline, Oct. 23, 1943
(39) Letter from Emil to Edward and Pauline, Oct. 25, 1943
(40) Letter from Emil to Paul and Nance, Oct. 6, 1944

# CHAPTER 16
## "Two Graves but No Regrets"
## 1944 – 1946

### A RACE WELL WON

Emil ran his race well, and he ended it well. He reached the finish line on November 7, 1944, at sixty-five years of age.

He never earned a college degree, never owned property, and never amassed earthly possessions. While many of his fellow missionaries had by this time purchased automobiles, Emil was still content to make his long safaris by motorcycle or, as he termed it, by leg-o-mobile.

The only legacy he left was a strong African church, a wealth of translated Scripture portions and other literature, and the strong example of a life fully devoted to his Master.

Marie described the circumstances of his final illness and death in a long letter to Paul and Nance:

> Before this reaches you, you will have received word and be waiting for further word. I know the news was a great shock to you. However much prayer has gone and is going up for you for the Lord's all-sustaining grace. I did not write before, for I knew how hard the uncertainty would have been on you— suspense is a better word.
>
> I know that you want to know all about your father's illness. It is difficult to write all about it. Your father has been weary in body, but of late has gone to bed quite early and now and then stayed in bed for an hour or two in the morning. As you know, I was always so glad for this.
>
> Sunday morning, October 29th, he came in while the rest of us were at breakfast, seemingly all right. After greetings, etc., I noticed he put his hand over his eyes more than the usual time.

184

*I think he must have felt badly then. After breakfast I asked if
he was going to Ngombe, as planned. He said, "Yes, I think I
will". So I asked about lunch. "Yes, I will take a little."*

*In a little while he kissed me goodbye and started off on the
motorcycle, seemingly all right. He had his meeting at
Ngombe, eleven miles out and another call at another place.
On his way home in the late afternoon, he was taken suddenly
ill with severe pain over the heart region. He was about six
miles from home at the time and he got off the motorcycle and
lay in the grass along the roadside. In about ten or fifteen
minutes an Indian station wagon came along and the men
picked him up and brought him here, and from here right to
the hospital. Your father requested this. He was suffering
greatly and could only tell me of the pain in the chest. Mr.
Ebeling was here and I asked him to get in the car and go to
the hospital while I stayed here to pick up a few necessities for
his personal hospital use and then went down.*

*I had prayed that your father might have the necessary
attention at once. Dr. Farr was still there and all did their best
for him at once. He was so dangerously ill that they did not
remove underwear and shirt for more than a day. The
diagnosis was a heart thrombosis. The two doctors made the
same diagnosis. You know what all of this meant. I need not
tell you. I, also, knew. The good doctor said the situation was
very grave and requested that I stay at the hospital. Of course,
I longed to do this. After forty-eight hours there was a change
for the better and the doctor thought that father had turned the
corner in the road to recovery. All knowing, of course, that
there would probably be another attack sooner or later—
maybe months or some years away. There was a slight but
steady improvement for two or three days. Then a slight turn
for the worse again Sunday morning, November 5th, and then
a decided turn for the worse on Monday. The hospital people
let me stay right on in spite of hospital rules as to visiting
hours — "Because it is you." I did so appreciate this and
spent the nights there and came home for meals during the
day...*

*He grew gradually worse and all knew that the end might
come any time. I stayed at your father's bedside, sending a
note home concerning the turn for the worse. At a quarter to
one, Monday night, the poor tired heart ceased to beat. I did*

*not call any of the staff when the end was near. I wanted those last precious minutes alone with him and they were precious. A little gasp or two and he was gone. "Absent from the body" — "Present with the Lord" — just that quick — no dark valley between. Yes, it hurt this last parting and while the tears rained down my cheeks, I could only say, "I thank you, Jesus, Oh Jesus, I thank You. I thank You." It seemed as though when the gates opened to your father that some of heaven's glory burst through and covered my heart. It is too sacred to describe, but it brought blessed heart-rest, peace and joy— past understanding—but very real—Wonderful Saviour!*

*We had sent wires in various directions to fellow missionaries in Tanganyika Territory and Kenya, as well as word by letter and on foot and through all of those trying days I felt wonderfully upheld through the ministry of the prayers of Europeans and Africans. "Blest be the tie that binds our hearts in love." Mr. Ebeling had come in and had to stay on in bed because of a slightly strained heart, not serious at all. Then Mr. Morrow came from Busia in a military lorry (last week). Mr. Baker came in from Nassa. So they saw to everything. We had the funeral yesterday in the late afternoon. First we had a service here in the church and then in a body our people walked to the European cemetery, the African pallbearers stopping at the hospital for your father's body. There was a nice casket (for Africa) and some friends had sent flowers. Mr. Baker had charge of the service at the grave in English and Mr. Morrow and Mr. Ebeling in Sukuma in the church. Our people feel all of this keenly. I trust it may mean revival in many a needy heart. God has many ways of working.*

*The men are making out an inventory of our belongings, etc., which must be handed in at the Boma. The will was handed in today. All this according to law. There is considerable money in the Bank, nearly all being from Mother's estate, and some Mission funds. This will be frozen for a bit until things are settled legally. I will not be in want meanwhile. I have some money here and, if need be, the Mission would forward money. Some will be coming in from bookshop sales, too. So don't give yourself any concern. The Lord will continue to supply. As to future plans, I hope to stay on here until the Lord makes His will known and shows the path. He will not fail me in this. Meanwhile I should like to have Mr. Ebeling here again. He*

*knows the lay of the land here in Mwanza and outschools and
the mission affairs in general. However, above all, we want
God's choice.*

*I am writing this way in the night. Folks have called here all
the hours of the day and of course, I must sit with them awhile.
Folks will probably be coming in from the outstations
tomorrow and for some time to come. One man gave me a
shilling towards hospital expenses and a woman gave me two
shillings. She came with her wee girl who cried all night
because the pastor was here no longer. Touching, isn't it? We
hope to hear from you soon by letter.*

*Remember, I am still in the need of prayer. The God of all
comfort be your portion as He is mine. With tender love, your
mother, Marie Sywulka. (1)*

## A NEW ROLE

The days following Emil's death were so demanding that
Marie was unable to mail the letter immediately. After some time,
she sat down and added a postscript describing her own
adjustments. She had come to Africa as a single missionary. Now,
past seventy, she was a single missionary again:

*I am sorry that we did not get this mailed sooner. There have
been many hitches these days. First of all I want to say that my
gracious Lord is upholding and sustaining me in a way I
cannot describe. Since the above was written a Council
meeting has been held here. I am to stay on and Mr. Ebeling
comes back to live here. There will, of necessity, be changes
later on but not right away. Quite a number of our
missionaries have come in. Mrs. Manning was a real help in
every way. Many letters have been received as well as
telegrams from our own and other societies as well as from
Africans. All feel the loss keenly. The cablegram to Betty was
a great shock to her. I have a long letter from her. She too
knows that all of God's ways are perfect and is resting in His
love. A little more about my private affairs lest you be over
concerned. Your father left everything to me. There are no old
debts as your father paid promptly. Books etc. just received
for the bookshop must be paid for. The Mission Treasurer paid
for the funeral and other associated expenses. We also had to*

*pay to the Government a tax according to things invoiced and
valued. I will be able to pay for all this as soon as things are
settled and I be given the right to draw funds from the Bank.
In with our money is considerable Mission money with Church
funds, pay for teacher-evangelists, etc. These sums must be put
into other hands now. After all these items are taken care of, I
will still have some money left. And I feel sure that my Father
will continue to meet all my need even as He has hitherto. To
Him all the praise! I wish that I could talk to you face to face
instead of write. There is so much to say. The Lord bless you
as He alone can bless. Mother (2)*

Marie sent a similar letter to Edward, describing in detail her
husband's illness, his death, and her own adjustments. Because of
war-time delays, it took three months for the sad news to reach
Guatemala. When the letter arrived, Edward was attending church
sessions in another town. Only after he returned home and read his
mother's words did he learn what had happened.

### ANOTHER LOSS—THE WHITLOCKS

With God's help, Marie found the strength to carry on. But
there were more blows yet to come.

Hard on the heels of her husband's death came the sad news of
fellow missionaries Paul and Helen Whitlock. They were on their
way back to Africa after a furlough, when their plane crashed off
the coast of South America. Their bodies were retrieved and buried
in Trinidad. Marie wrote to Ed and Pauline:

*Today I am trying to get letters off to my three children. How
far apart we are from one another—scattered far and wide. I
praise the Lord that the distance to the throne of grace is the
same for each one of us. May we meet there often.*

*I suppose that you have written to Betty... She has been ill
again. Poor, poor child. It is first one thing and then another
and all serious illnesses too. I know that the Lord who has
seen her through six troubles will see her through the
seventh...*

*Your letter to us... showed that it had come in contact with
water... The stamp had soaked off. Also marked, "Air mail via
Clipper."... All feel certain that this was salvaged mail from*

*the clipper on which our Whitlocks perished... The Whitlocks
started their journey for Africa and ended it in the haven of
rest in Immanuel's land. I like to think that your father was at
one of the pearly gates to welcome them. Had I written that
the Whitlocks were to be stationed in Mwanza. A letter
addressed to your father and written by Mr. Whitlock reached
here four days ago. He had enclosed keys for trunks and lists
of contents of boxes to present at Customs here...*

*The California people sent me some money—telegraphed it...
Monies from Brooklyn were put in my name after they
received the cable from here. The Lord has been so very good
to me. "Great is Thy Faithfulness." He continues to be my
comfort and my all sufficient portion in every sense of the
word. My strength and my song. I thank Him that so far I have
been able to stay on here in Mwanza. I feel quite well but am a
bit weary. (3)*

## *"Betty is Worse Again."*

Although Marie thanked God that she could stay on in
Mwanza, her heart went out to her children so far away—
especially Paul in the armed forces, and Betty so unwell.

For fourteen years Marie had ministered to other families as
they came and went through Mwanza. Now she longed to minister
to her own children. She had counted on the Whitlocks to take over
the Mwanza work, but the Lord had called them to Himself in the
plane crash. It was only after the arrival of the Russell Bakers—
eight months after Emil's death—that Marie felt free to visit Betty.
She wrote to Edward and Pauline:

*So many times I thank the Lord that though we as a family are
scattered to the far ends of the earth, the distance to the throne
of our God is the same. I have had no word concerning Paul
for many, many weeks. I sometimes wonder if he is in the Far
East by now or still in Europe somewhere. My Father knows
and that is enough...*

*I am feeling much better again. Now since the Bakers have
been stationed here to carry on the Mwanza work I felt free to
make some plans concerning the future. I asked the Council
for permission to go to South Africa for an indefinite time. (4)*

The Council gave its permission, but not so the government offices. Shortly after World War II ended, Marie wrote to Nance, who was bravely raising the two boys alone, while Paul remained overseas:

> *I do so want to hear from Betty and Stephen again. Betty writes that she is worse again. Stephen writes the same. Poor, poor girl. I long to be with her. So far the necessary government papers for entrance to South Africa have not been received. It takes time and patience...*
>
> *I suppose that Paul is still with the forces in Germany. I long to know. (5)*

The days stretched into long months, and still the South Africa visa was denied. Marie wrote to Emil's brother Edward:

> *Letters from Emil's family are always appreciated though I am just an in-law. The Lord keeps you in my heart and all are remembered daily before the Father.*
>
> *Betty's health is still far from what it should be. Poor girl, she needs your prayers. When the way opens I will be going to her to help lift burdens. There is so much red tape to unwind in order to get into South Africa. It takes time and patience. We still have a God who can and will make a way where there is no way.*
>
> *Edward and Pauline have four children. Wee Dora was born in May. I have reason to believe that Edward and Pauline are real missionaries. My prayer is that Emil's mantle fall upon Edward's shoulders.*
>
> *Paul is still in Germany attached to General Eisenhower's headquarters. I trust that the family will be reunited soon. Paul and Nance have two small sons.*
>
> *I keep going but do feel my age. I praise God for the service He has granted us in Africa. Never, for one moment, have I regretted obeying the call to service. His "Lo I am with you always" has been, is, and will continue to be blessedly true. (6)*

### SOUTH AFRICA AT LAST

By late November 1945, more than a year after Emil's death, Marie was in Kijabe and her passage to South Africa appeared more hopeful. She wrote to Paul and Nance:

*I came here Nov. 23rd. Left home the 20th. It was a bit hard to leave our Africans after being a part of them for fourteen years in Mwanza and outstations. However, God's grace is always sufficient. The same is true concerning the grave. Here too His peace is sufficient plus "that blessed hope" which is ours who belong to Christ and look for His coming again when the graves of the saints will give up their prey and we with them shall be "forever with the Lord." "Perhaps today."*

*Nearly all AIM stations and those of other Societies, too, are seriously undermanned and not a few closed for lack of workers. Our Mwanza station has no resident man missionary. Mr. Stier will come over from Usinza Station every two weeks or so to oversee the mission affairs. The Guest House is in charge of Miss Hayes, and Miss Upham has charge of work among women and children. I am so sorry that there is no one for the outstation work as well as colportage work. You will know how to pray.*

*The agents wrote that I might have to embark from Mombasa, Kenya, as a ship might not stop at our Tanganyika port, Dar-es-Salaam. I wanted to be on the safe side so came to Kenya and will stay here at Kijabe until the way opens for me to go to South Africa. When, I do not know, but I trust it will be soon. Betty needs me. I think that I am in the priority list, having been in East Africa for fourteen years without furlough. However, military men returning to South Africa have and should have priority. Well, your Father knoweth and He will not fail to open the way for me in His own way and right time. We have a great God who still doeth wonders. (7)*

By early 1946, Marie was finally in South Africa. To her sorrow, she found that Betty's condition was rapidly growing worse. She and Stephen urged Betty to let them take her to the hospital, but Betty at first was completely unwilling to leave her home.

**1946 - Betty, Steve, Marie, Maud and Herbert Barrett, Miss Green.**
*Front:* **Grace Marie and Elizabeth Ann Barrett**

When Betty finally relented, not a single hospital in Durban would admit her. The large T. B. hospital had a waiting list of over 150 patients, and all the others were also full.

At last Stephen learned that he could get his wife into a hospital in Pietermaritzburg, 100 miles away. Saying a tearful goodbye to her mother and daughters, Betty got into the auto with her husband and his friend Henry Hawkins, and they drove away.

Three days later, Stephen and Henry were back in Durban to pick up Marie and the girls so they could see Betty on her thirty-third birthday. From Pietermaritzburg, Marie wrote to Edward and Pauline:

> *The lung condition is hopeless as well as the diabetes. It was so hard for her to say goodbye to us, especially the little children when she left home. But she has been very brave through all her suffering...*
>
> *Stephen and Henry came home again after three days, and all started for here the next day, her birthday. We wanted her to have her family here for that. We bought her some lovely*

*flowers. A birthday cake was out of the question. I am staying on here, probably until our gracious Lord calls Betty home to the blessed Glory Land. Stephen and the children left yesterday for home... I am so glad that I can be with Betty these days and that I have the privilege of doing little things for her like giving her hair a good brushing... and comfort from the Old Book, etc. I praise God too that I am within walking distance of the Hospital, about 17 minutes walk. Major and Mrs. Usher of the Salvation Army have opened their lovely home to us. The Lord reward them. (8)*

## A SECOND GRAVE IN AFRICA

Betty died on June 30, 1946. Once again, Marie sat down to inform her sons of a Sywulka grave. Once again, she described in detail the circumstances of a loved one's passing and expressed her own unshakable faith.

She wrote the following letter to Edward and asked him to pass it on to Paul:

*I know that you will be waiting for a letter from me. Before this reaches you, you will have had word from Paul telling you of your sister's Home call to the Glory Land. I sent the cable to him, and asked that he notify you, Akron, and the California relatives. I know that in a way you were prepared for the news. We had prayed much that the Lord would get our hearts ready, especially Stephen's father and mother, who had so looked forward to having Stephen, Betty and the children with them. Even built an addition to the house for them. They are real lovers of the Lord. Well, Betty has gone to her Heavenly Home where the many mansions are. Didn't Jesus say, "I go to prepare a place for you that where I am there you may be also". It is such a comfort to know that she is at rest and with Christ which is far better. No more suffering, no more pain, no more sleepless nights. Blessed release. She suffered so much in various ways these past months. I marvel that her poor sick body stood the suffering as long as it did. Day by day our Father gave the extra strength and courage needed.*

*How very glad I am that I could be with her these last six months of her life and especially the past weeks here in Maritzburg where she was in Hospital. Betty had a bad spell June 27th but felt better again later on in the day. Saturday*

*June 29th I had a call from the Hospital saying that Betty had had a very bad night and was worse. "Shall I send for her husband?" "Yes, I would" was the answer. To get a long distance message through to a place four miles from the Mission Station, they got a man off on horseback at once. Stephen began to get ready at once. It meant getting himself and the children ready to stay awhile, arranging for the care of the station, etc., and he reached here about 7 p.m. Meanwhile I was spending the day with Betty doing little services for her. She was very weak...*

*Stephen saw her that evening Saturday. Talked to her a bit and had prayer with her. She had a smile for him when he said goodnight. Next morning Sunday there was an urgent call from the Hospital saying that Betty was very ill. Stephen went to the Hospital while I looked after the children's breakfast as Major and Mrs. Usher were on safari. Stephen came back for me in a little while...*

*I saw at once that our Betty was indeed very sick and the end not far off. They were giving her oxygen...*

*Not long after that Betty said, "I want to go Home." Stephen answered, "You are going home, Betty dear." She seemed to lose consciousness shortly after that... and in a moment or two the old over-tired heart gave up the struggle... "Absent from the body, present with the Lord." Just that quick and no dark valley between. How safe she is in the presence of her Lord and how happy. Oh the bliss of seeing her Saviour face to face as well as being reunited with her loved ones gone on before...*

*The funeral service was held at the Baptist Church here... The congregation sang, "My Jesus I love Thee," Long ago Betty requested this. So long ago that Stephen almost forgot...*

*I knew that you, Paul, and the Akron relatives would have sent flowers if you could have. So I did it for you—a wreath from you, one from Paul and one from the Akron folk and marked accordingly. Betty had flowers all the time she was in Hospital. Some from far distant places like Capetown ordered through florists elsewhere and purchased here like in USA. The flowers gave her much pleasure. The Lord raised up many friends for her and for me too. How kind and good these friends have been to us strangers in a strange place...*

*As the Ushers will be away from home much of the time, it meant asking the Lord to find a place for me elsewhere. One day at Hospital, Mr. Herringshaw said that they would be away from July 1st to 26th. Would we like to stay there meanwhile? So here we are, the children and I and Stephen... This is the Lord's doing and it is marvelous in our eyes.*

*The little girls did not see their mother again after coming down this time. We did not take them to church nor the cemetery. We told them that Mama would not be coming home but that she had gone to be with Jesus. They do not mourn for her. Grace is five years old and Elizabeth four. They are well and happy. I will help in their care here and when we go back to the mission station near the end of the month. Stephen left this morning for Zululand where there is the regular yearly gathering for mission business. (9)*

## Caring for Betty's Girls

Sensing that that her granddaughters needed her, Marie remained for some time in South Africa. She enjoyed mothering them and seeing her son-in-law's work among the Zulu people. Even though she lost her husband, her daughter, her sister Anna and her sister-in-law Emma in less than two years, she hadn't forgotten how to praise the Lord, nor how to enjoy music and flowers. From Rockmount, Natal, she wrote to Edward:

*Blossom time is past and roses are in full bloom. Garden planted. I am glad that it is warmer again.*

*The station school is next door. Over 100 attend. There are three teachers. Just now there is a lot of singing going on. I do like to hear the Zulu sing. Miss Botterill has taken over the Bible study classes. Also women's work.*

*By now you have heard of Aunt Emma's home call... Aunt Emma, Aunt Anna, Betty and your father in less than two years. "As for God, His way is perfect." Continue to pray for us. I know you do. (10)*

Marie hadn't lost her love of cooking, either. She wrote again:

*Yesterday was Thanksgiving Day. I find that I have so much to be thankful for. I praise Him that He accepts the sacrifice of praise. The past year has had its sore testings and trials but God's grace has been all sufficient and He has been a very present help in trouble and the God of all comfort. To Him all the praise.*

*I had a special dinner for my family. Roast beef with Yorkshire pudding, bread, sweet potatoes, whole onions burned with meat, gravy, buttered string beans, pumpkin pie made with sweet potatoes, nuts and marshmallows. Also baked a big spice layer cake the day before. We have to make our cakes and all baked goods with unsifted whole wheat flour as white flour is not to be had. Stephen and I went to Pietermartizburg last Thursday p.m. and returned Monday evening. I was anxious to see Betty's grave as I had not seen it since it was taken care of. We miss her more than tongue can tell. What a comfort to know that all is well with her. We shall miss her so much this coming Christmas. I am planning on making it a special day for Stephen and the wee girlies...*

*The rainy season is on. I wish that you could see the great variety of wild flowers including calla lilies—white, yellow and blood-red! Our garden is doing very well. We have plenty of milk, butter and eggs. The Lord is good. There is a real lack in South Africa of tea, rice, butter for people that have to buy it, and sugar too, and most of all soap due to lack of soap fats. Elizabeth and Grace love to wash dolly clothes and need lots of soap but we give them a wee bit that must last a long time. (11)*

## RETURN TO AMERICA

Instead of returning to Mwanza, Marie felt she should accompany Stephen and the girls to America. Once they were settled with Stephen's parents—Maurice and Grace Barrett in Missouri—she could think about returning to Tanganyika.

Stephen tried to arrange passage in late 1946, but the boat agencies told him he would have to wait until March of the following year, or even later. Miraculously, passage was arranged by the end of January 1947. From Durban, Marie wrote a hasty note to Edward:

*Just to say that D. V. we leave here for New York tomorrow on the S. S.* Garden State *and should reach New York about February 15th, making only one stop at Port of Spain, Trinidad...*

*We were on the boat this a. m. and I and the kiddies have a lovely cabin. The table was set for lunch and I saw a plate of* white bread! *After all, I like brown bread the best. (12)*

By late February, Marie was once again in America. From Ferguson, Missouri, she wrote to Edward and Pauline, describing the month-long voyage with its disappointments and unexpected provisions:

*Here I am in the home of Stephen's people!... We left January 26th, spending two days in Durban... We sailed direct to Trinidad casting anchor about three miles from port. I did so want to visit the graves of our Whitlock family. No one went ashore. Water and oil was brought to us.*

*After a day or so away from Trinidad the captain was informed by radio that we were to land at Pensacola, Florida, instead of "up north." It was rather disturbing to all concerned. Three passengers were headed for Canada. It meant a lot of extra and unlooked for expenses.*

*Then next day another message to the captain informed him that due to the inconvenience caused to passengers, the States Marine Corps would pay the railway fares of passengers to their destinations. We got off the boat on Tuesday 18th February. Stephen saw to all business affairs also visited one or two Columbia Bible College people living and in work there [in Pensacola]. At 12:45 p.m. a railway truck was at the docks for trunks etc. and a car... provided to take us to the Station. "Measure pressed down, shaken together and running over." Jesus never fails. Even came to St. Louis by Pullman. We got here Wednesday near morning.*

*Stephen's parents were here to meet us. Stephen was away for nine years and the folks had never seen the little girls. Maybe you can imagine the little family scenes. Naturally we all thought of Betty not being with us.*

*I, too, was given a warm welcome and a warm house, rather important to me. The children are causing the same excitement that you children caused in 1913. I had no thought of coming here until we had the message about landing in Pensacola. Stephen urged me to come. I am not certain of how many days I will be here, then on to Paul and by and by to Ohio. Naturally Ohio is home town. I will miss Aunt Anna most of all. She had asked me to make my home with her and I had it in my heart to do so. There will be no Uncle Henry either as well as no Uncle Zeph and Aunt Emma. Time has made many changes. (13)*

Marie, satisfied that Stephen's parents would do a fine job of raising the girls, stayed in Missouri only a few days. Speaking opportunities began popping up immediately, the first being a conference at Betty's home congregation—Calvary Church of Lancaster, Pennsylvania. From Ferguson, Marie wrote to Emil's brother Edward:

*I know that I am putting the little motherless girls into good hands. Stephen and I leave this week for a great missionaries conference held in Lancaster, Pennsylvania, March 2 - 9. Missionaries from all societies will be there. Pray. Betty was a member of the church where the conference will be held and [she was] their first missionary. I left two graves in Africa but have no regrets. I count it all joy. (14)*

It became an oft-repeated refrain in the years to come. Time and again Marie would say, "I have two graves in Africa, but no regrets." And she meant it with all her heart.

### References

(1)  Letter from Marie to Paul and Nance, November 8, 1944
(2)  *Ibid.*
(3)  Letter from Marie to Edward and Pauline, Feb. 23, 1945
(4)  Letter from Marie to Edward and Pauline, July 26, 1945
(5)  Letter from Marie to Nance, Sept 10, 1945
(6)  Letter from Marie to Edward and Nora Gray, Nov. 1, 1945
(7)  Letter from Marie to Paul and Nance, Nov. 29, 1945
(8)  Letter from Marie to Edward and Pauline, May 1946
(9)  Letter from Marie to Edward and Paul, July 5, 1946
(10) Letter from Marie to Edward and Pauline, Oct. 18, 1946
(11) Letter from Marie to Edward and Pauline, Nov. 30, 1946
(12) Letter from Marie to Edward and Pauline, Jan. 25, 1947
(13) Letter from Marie to Edward and Pauline, 21 Feb. 1947
(14) Letter from Marie to Edward and Nora Gray, 24 Feb. 1947

# Chapter 17
## Back to Africa at Seventy-Five
## 1947 – 1949

### *WINFIELD, ILLINOIS*

After the conference in Pennsylvania, Marie traveled to Winfield, Illinois, to visit her son Paul. She had not seen him in sixteen years! And she had never before met Nance and the two young grandsons.

While at Paul's, she also wanted to meet the young married couples' class at Wheaton's College Church. She was most eager to thank them for their part in her support. Through the influence of Paul and Nance, this Sunday school class had been faithfully sending her five dollars each month.

Emil's brother Edward and his wife Nora made a special trip to visit Marie while she was with her son Paul. How glad she was that they wanted to keep in touch even though Emil was gone.

Eventually, she also hoped to see her son Edward, for his furlough was coinciding with hers. It would be her first face-to-face acquaintance with Pauline, although the two felt they knew each other well through long years of exchanging letters. And she wanted to get to know Edward's children. From Paul's home, she wrote to Emil's brother:

> *For the present I am here with Paul and family. I do not know as to the future. I know the Lord will make it plain and lead step by step. I want to be in His will. I remember Emil saying, "To be in the will of God is to be in the sweetest place this side of heaven."*
>
> *Edward and family reached Dallas, Texas, recently. They came by plane from Guatemala. Tomorrow, no—today—they are due to be in Norman, Oklahoma to attend the Summer*

199

*School of Linguistics. I rather think Edward will be doing
some teaching as well as further training along Mam
language lines. One of the hardest if not the hardest of Indian
languages. They want me to be with them if there is room.
Students come first. Naturally I long to see these dear ones.
Norman seems so far away, and the cost of travel is quite an
item as well as other expenses involved. Time will tell. (1)*

## AKRON, OHIO

Six months later, Marie had still not been able to get to
Oklahoma. But she was enjoying her sister Lizzie's hospitality in
Akron. She wrote to Emil's brother:

*I am glad that you were still planning on a visit to Edward and
family. I am writing this to tell you that I am thinking of you
and that I do so appreciate seeing you in Winfield. Also to
wish you a blessed Christmas season, in your own home I
hope, and blessing in full measure from above for the New
Year.*

*"He goeth before." I am with my sister, R. 4, Box 666, Akron
1, Ohio, and will probably stay here for some weeks to come.
(2)*

## NORMAN, OKLAHOMA

A year after arriving in the States, Marie finally had the joy of
seeing Edward and meeting his family for the first time. They had
extended their furlough so that Edward could get an M.A. in
linguistics at the University of Oklahoma.

Marie had always loved children, and here were five
grandchildren for her to enjoy all at once! She delighted in the
creativity of the older three who seemed to produce a constant flow
of drawings, songs, stories, and childish rhymes.

Then there were the two who were born after Emil's death:
Dora, a pre-schooler; and Betty Sue, still a baby. Marie bustled
about from dawn to dusk, baking special German sweets for the
older children and rocking the baby to sleep. Betty Sue was

Marie's ninth grandchild, and the only one she had seen as an infant.

**Marie with Betty Sue**

## SAD NEWS FROM MISSOURI

Marie returned to Akron, her heart full of happy memories. But there was sadness, too. Her son-in-law Stephen Barrett had been diagnosed with a rapidly advancing form of leukemia. Her sister Lizzie and niece Gertrude had been to St. Louis, had seen the Barretts, and had brought her a fresh report on his condition. She wrote to Edward and Pauline:

> *Of course they had to find the house. They saw two little girls playing in the yard and spoke to them. "One looked so much like Betty." That was Grace. Soon they met the rest of the family. They had a nice visit with Stephen and it meant so much to him to see them. Naturally there were some tears. Before they left, Stephen had to be taken to the doctor for treatment, his brother taking him...*

*Next Sunday I speak at a church in Cleveland. Remember me*
*in prayer. I want these opportunities to count. (3)*

And to Emil's brother, she wrote the following:

*I have had no very recent word concerning Stephen. He was a*
*bit better again after a run of high temperature, 105 degrees,*
*for days. My sister with whom I am staying and my niece made*
*a few hours stop-over in St. Louis recently and called on the*
*Barretts. I am so glad that at last they met the girlies and*
*Stephen. It meant much to Stephen too. I did not make a visit*
*to St. Louis on my way home from Norman as I had to hurry*
*back to Ohio. Keep on praying for Stephen. I am sure we want*
*God's will in this matter, knowing that always God's way is*
*the perfect and best way. He is so needed among the Zulus.*

*I still do not know as to when I will be returning to Africa.*
*Boat passage is so very costly these days. "Your Father*
*knoweth" and will meet the need in His own time and way. My*
*department of work had to shut doors for lack of the necessary*
*help. So pray if the Lord so leads. (4)*

## A BUSY SPEAKING SCHEDULE

Back in Akron, Marie kept busy. In her seventy-fifth year
now, her energy was still unabated. She kept up a busy
correspondence with in-laws, nieces and nephews as well as with
her sons and grandchildren. Most weekends she was on the go with
speaking engagements; she reported to Edward that she had only
been to her home church, Calvary Evangelical, twice. "Other
Sundays I have been out of town in meetings." (5)

Her heart-strings seemed pulled in so many directions! She
wished she could peek in on the three little families in Winfield,
Norman, and St. Louis, where she was especially concerned about
Stephen. But most of all her heart was pulled back toward
Mwanza. That was where she belonged, and she was glad for every
open door to present Africa's need:

*I do not hear from the Barretts… Stephen is not able to write*
*and I cannot expect it of his mother. There are too many other*
*demands on her strength and time, caring for the girlies,*

202

*Stephen needing care and much else... So many people ask about Stephen through letters and in conversation. How I long to know how he is these days. I'm glad that I can pray for him and the family. Stephen and the children certainly pull at my heart strings.*

*Now a word about safari plans... The plan so far has been that I leave for Pennsylvania some time after the middle of August, make a stop over in Pittsburgh and Lancaster... then on to Christ's Home. If they still have their yearly over-Labor-Day meetings I want to be there. (6)*

*We do want the Lord to order our steps, our coming and going, don't we. We know He has a plan and waits to work out that plan.*

*I had word the other day that our dear Mr. Schwab has departed this life. Christ's Home will not be the same to me without Mr. Schwab. I wonder who will take his place as head of the place.*

*October 19-28th I go with a group of several women to have part in their Fall Missionary Institutes. I will be the Missionary speaker and be on the program twice a day for eight institutes. After that I have no definite plans. (7)*

## STEPHEN BARRETT'S DEATH

While on a five-weeks speaking tour in Pennsylvania, Marie learned that Betty's husband lost his battle with leukemia on September 14, 1948.

The big question on everyone's mind was: Who will care for Steve and Betty's girls? Emil's brother Edward Gray and his wife wondered whether they could take Grace and Elizabeth into their childless home, but Marie tactfully let them know that the decision was not up to her:

*I have not heard what plans were made between Stephen and his parents concerning the children. I feel quite certain that the Barretts will continue caring for the children even as they have in the past. They are very fond of the little girlies and all the more so since they had no girls of their own and with*

*Stephen's death they will feel that more than ever before, they want to give the children the heart love and devotion—dear motherless and fatherless darlings. My heart goes out to them. I too wish that I could care for them. I'm glad you wrote to the Barretts.*

*Stephen's death is another hard blow. I still cannot think it true. I am so glad for him, "Absent from the body, present with the Lord." "With Christ which is far better." My heart's cry is, who will fill the gap in the ranks over there in Zululand? Stephen was a fine missionary. He did not meet his Lord empty-handed. I am sure his Zulu brethren feel the loss too. Little did we think when we left South Africa that Stephen would not return. "As for God, His way is perfect."*

*And now the Lord bless you and reward you for your kind thought and desire to take in as your very own two of the tender Shepherd's lambs. (8)*

## PASSPORT PICTURES AND SHOTS

In the end, it seemed best for the Barrett grandparents to keep the girls. Marie tried to assuage the Grays' disappointment. She also informed them of her plans to return to Africa:

*Here I am at home again after being away four days this week and four days last week going about from place to place with a group of women helping in their Fall Missionary Rallies. I was the guest speaker, speaking twice a day. The Lord undertook and again verified that when He gives us a task to do, He also gives us the wherewith to do it...*

*So far I have not heard from the Barretts concerning the children. From what Edward said, it seems that they plan to keep the children though Stephen had not mentioned concerning the care of the children. I trust that you have had a letter from Mrs. Barrett long before this. I still think it was very fine in you to offer the help you did...*

*This coming week I plan to have passport pictures taken. Then apply for passport. I must also see to various shots for typhus, typhoid, tetanus, smallpox and yellow fever. The last named not obtainable here but in New York later on. There must also*

*be a re-entrance to East Africa permit, visa, etc. The big*
*problem is getting passage on a boat. All of this stretches over*
*a period of many weeks. So keep on praying and praising too.*
*As things work out, I'll write to you from time to time. (9)*

Surrounded by relatives in Akron, Marie celebrated her
seventy-fifth birthday—then Christmas—and all the while she was
still waiting for her re-entry permit. It was a familiar pattern by
now; never had permission been granted swiftly and easily, but
never had she failed to trust God to open the way:

*I have been looking for my re-entry permit to Tanganyika.*
*Yesterday I had a letter from the Home Office saying that*
*word has been received that there is a new law (they happen*
*overnight) and that papers from Tanganyika Territory will be*
*sent to me to fill out and to return the same airmail. So we*
*must go through the whole procedure again. I am so sorry*
*about the delay. A matter of from thirty to sixty days or more.*
*"Your Father knoweth" and "God is faithful." (10)*

The new year—1949—came in, the Akron relatives put on a
goodbye party, and Calvary Church gave Marie a farewell. In faith,
but without her permit, she headed for in Brooklyn in February.
Here she wrote:

*I found a lot of missionaries [in New York]. In fact, 26 people*
*counting children all awaiting for delayed boats to sail... I am*
*still waiting for the re-entry permit. "Stand still and see the*
*salvation of the Lord." (11)*

At last everything came together: the re-entry permit, the
sailing date, the passage money. Once again, after weeks and
months of standing still, Marie witnessed the parting of her own
personal Red Sea. She left March 29, 1949, hoping to reach
Capetown by mid-April. (12)

Her plan was to make a long stopover in South Africa, so that
she could visit Stephen and Betty's co-workers. After that she'd
board another ship, which would land her in Mombasa by May.
From a mission home in Durban, she wrote to her son Paul:

*Arrived here April 27th. Miss Botterill who was with us on*
*Stephen's station met me... Passed through Estcourt only 24*
*miles from where we lived. Naturally memories flooded heart*

205

*and mind. Also as we passed through Maritzburg. "Sorrowful yet rejoicing" knowing that "God's way is perfect."*

*My boat is in and was to leave tomorrow but there is a dock strike on since this a.m. ... I have met so many fine people here, coming and going. I think there were 31 yesterday. (13)*

Despite the dock strike, Marie reached Nairobi by the middle of May. She wrote to Edward and Pauline:

*Well here I am in Kenya. I landed at Mombasa the 13th. Agents helped me with customs etc. You will be glad to know that there were no customs charges. I thank the Lord for this. The agents' clerk, a black man, said, "They were good to you because you are an old lady."*

*You would not know Nairobi. It is quite a city, well planned and flowers everywhere and lovely homes instead of being a "tin town" as in 1906. "Tin" means corrugated iron sheets. Schools, hospitals, churches for all races. Lovely shops too. Tomorrow there is a women's meeting here. I am to give a little message. My topic: Praise changes things...*

*I will reach Mwanza early Monday morning, Lord willing, and get to the mission station in time for breakfast. Miss Tilley assures me a big welcome—black and white—at the landing. Hitherto the Lord hath helped all along the way. (14)*

Once again, Marie was back in Africa. Back in Africa, where she belonged.

---

**References:**

(1)  Letter from Marie to Edward and Nora Gray, June 2, 1947
(2)  Letter from Marie to Edward and Nora Gray, Dec. 17, 1947
(3)  Letter from Marie to Edward and Pauline, June 23, 1948
(4)  Letter from Marie to Edward and Nora Gray, June 23, 1948
(5)  Letter from Marie to Edward and Pauline, July 18, 1948
(6)  Letter from Marie to Edward and Pauline, Aug. 4, 1948
(7)  Letter from Marie to Edward and Pauline, Aug. 15, 1948
(8)  Letter from Marie to Edward and Nora Gray, Oct. 4, 1948
(9)  Letter from Marie to Edward and Nora Gray, Oct. 30, 1948
(10) Letter from Marie to Edward and Nora Gray, Dec. 14, 1948
(11) Letter from Marie to Edward and Pauline, Feb. 22, 1949
(12) Letter from Marie to Edward and Pauline, March 28, 1949

(13) Letter from Marie to Paul, May 2, 1949
(14) Letter from Marie to Edward and Pauline, May 18, 1949

# CHAPTER 18
# Great is Thy Faithfulness
# 1949 – 1971

## *A WARM WELCOME*

Warmly welcomed back to Mwanza by both "black and white", Marie settled into the new, small cottage which her fellow missionaries had built especially for her. Soon she was back in her familiar routine: seeing to the comfort of people in the guest house, applying her nursing skills to the cuts and bruises of African school boys, and writing long letters to her far-flung family.

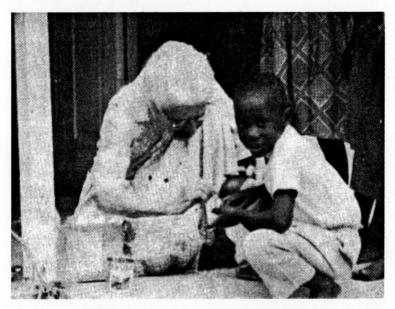

**Marie in Mwanza with a young patient**

## SAD AND HAPPY NEWS FROM GUATEMALA

Reading mail from her dear ones was a highlight of Marie's day. She liked to imagine how her grandchildren were growing and what they were learning.

Then came news that her youngest grandbaby had died in Guatemala, on August 19, 1949, after a brief illness. Marie recalled the happy days in Norman when she had rocked little Betty Sue. And she thought of her own Betty's grave, there in South Africa where she had so recently visited. With a heart full of emotion she wrote to Edward and Pauline:

> *This morning's mail brought me the airmail letter from Dallas telling me that our precious baby is with the Lord Jesus. Safe forever in His tender care and keeping. I bow my head and say, "I worship Thee, sweet will of God, and all Thy ways adore" knowing that "As for God, His way is perfect." How my heart goes out to you in this your great sorrow and loss. I know that you will find His grace so all sufficient and that "underneath are the everlasting arms." Also that your earthly loss will be translated into heavenly gain. The God of all comfort comfort your hearts and give you the wherewith to comfort other sorrowing hearts who pass through a like sorrow. It means so much to be able to say, "I know, I know. I, too, have been through this." (1)*

In 1950, Edward and Pauline had something more joyous to report. They wrote of "the arrival of Priscilla Ruth on Sept. 18 to join our happy family of little ones." (2) And in 1953, Philip Howard was born, making Edward's family complete with three boys and three girls. Marie now had five living grandsons and five living granddaughters.

## CHANGES AND GROWTH

The 1950 annual missionaries' conference meant extra work for Marie, since many passed through Mwanza both going and coming. When the last traveler had left, Marie paused to reflect on the changes Tanganyika had seen since the early days. Then she sat down to write to Edward and Pauline:

*All left for home on Monday. As usual a goodly number of people had to come here to go elsewhere. What a Monday. Quite a number had to spend the night here. Again the Lord undertook and met every need. I have just been thinking of the first Missionary Conference held in these parts long ago. Seven Church Missionary Society missionaries—all men in those days—met at Usambira. Three months later two of the men had laid down their lives there...*

*Very recently we held our AIM African Conference at Nera. This Conference is held every two years... Can you imagine nearly five thousand people attending? People brought their sleeping mats and food. A very temporary chapel of reeds, grass, etc. was put up. A loud speaker carried the messages to the rear and beyond. Again the trumpeters had a vital part in music and testimonies, these being translated into Sukuma.*

*I praise God for all that He has done for us here in our field during the years 1909 -1950. The seed sowing has not been in vain. The Lord has honored the giving out of the Word. To Him all the praise. However there is still much land to be possessed within and without and our hearts cry out for His "much more."*

*About time to close this letter. However I must tell you that the Guest House has a refrigerator! Received a few days ago from America. Our missionary family here sensed the real need so hearts and purses opened—gifts came in to Mr. Maynard and now we have the frig! I do praise the Lord. Mr. Dilworth, returning from a vacation through game country. Shot some and left plenty here. Now frozen hard as a rock and to be kept for emergencies. No longer must milk be boiled twice a day to keep it sweet. As we have electricity in Mwanza, the refrigerator is an electric one. Also have running water. Mwanza is quite a town and what a mission field! (3)*

## WORKERS TOGETHER WITH HIM

In the early 1950's, Marie added a new project to her busy schedule: writing up the history of the early days of mission work in Tanganyika.

For some time, her fellow missionaries had been begging for such a work. Many African Christians, too, came to her asking,

"We want the history of the early days. Pastor Sywulka is no longer with us, and you are the only one left to tell us." (4)

And so Marie set about very carefully to sort through Emil's papers, her own memories, and the recollections of older African friends. She made every effort to ensure that names and dates were correct, and finally sent off the manuscript to the AIM Press in Congo.

Her little 48-page booklet is undated, but brings the work up to "June, 1952." (5) It must have come off the presses in 1953 or 1954, for the editors added the following about the Mwanza Guest House, noting that the paragraph was added by them, and not Marie:

> At the 1953 Field Conference the name, Emmaus Guest
> House, was chosen officially by the missionary body; Em for
> "Dad" Emil Sywulka, Ma for Mother Marie Sywulka, the
> founders of this wonderful haven of rest. And us? Well, for just
> us; you and I, who often dirty, weary, worn and hungry, have
> come under the gracious care of the home makers. Often
> Mother Sywulka said, "You better eat before you go. One
> never knows what happens on safari." And how often this was
> a wise prophecy! (6)

### ANNIVERSARY CELEBRATIONS

Marie was growing older but she had no thought of leaving Africa. Shortly before turning 80 she wrote:

> I think Mrs. Stauffacher and I are the oldest or rather longest
> on the field. She in 1905 and I in 1906. As far as I know, I am
> the oldest in years. How wonderfully the Lord has undertaken
> for us all down the years (7).

Emil had never been one to celebrate birthdays, anniversaries and holidays. In fact, so occupied was he with his many duties, and so burdened for the spiritual condition of his parish, that he often forgot these occasions entirely. Marie, on the other hand, kept close track of the calendar and enjoyed celebrating God's faithfulness when special days came around. In July 1956, she took particular note of the fiftieth anniversary of her first arrival in Africa. The *Inland Africa* magazine reported:

*Of this half century of service she says: "A jubilee shall the
fiftieth year be unto you and so it is in every sense of the word.
To God be all the praise. Jesus Christ, the same yesterday,
today and forever." (8)*

Four years later, Marie was still celebrating that anniversary,
this time by giving out Scripture portions. She wrote to Edward
and Pauline:

*Today I purchased a lot of Gospels in Swahili —Matthew,
Mark, John— at our station bookshop. No Luke because they
never got here though sent.*

*July 17th or 19th, I forget the date, it will be 54 years ago that
I landed in Kenya. 54 years ago! And I am going to give out
these gospels as a token of praise and thanksgiving to our
great God for what He has done for me. Great is Thy
faithfulness. (9)*

## NEW PRINTING PRESS

When the AIM established a publishing center in Mwanza, it
seemed appropriate to ask Marie to cut the ribbon at its dedication.
The new building housed a late model offset press, as well as a
typesetting machine, process camera, power cutter and automatic
folder. Marie thought back to the days when Emil laboriously set
type by hand, turning many an "n" upside down so there would be
enough "u's" for Sukuma. Then she thought of the little hand press
on which, even earlier, he printed the Gospel of John. Now
everything would be printed with lightning speed on presses run by
electricity. (10)

## AFRICAN CHURCH JUBILEE

In 1959, the African Inland Church of Tanganyika celebrated
its golden jubilee. Nearly 29,000 tribal church members converged
in a great gathering. The African church leaders had asked Marie
to address the great crowd in the opening meeting, and she rose to
recount the wonderful works of God.

All eyes turned to the little 85-year-old woman on the platform. Her face was framed by her thick, curly white hair, and her brown eyes sparkled with great joy as she spoke of the early days. An AIM news brief stated: "How fitting that the African Church leaders should ask her to perform this service at the beginning of the conference." (11) And Marie herself wrote:

> *This conference was altogether under African control... A huge, very temporary shelter was put up where the services were held. Made of bamboo poles, corn stalks, tree branches, grasses, etc., and met the need. Other shelters were put up where people slept...*

> *People of all ages were there: gray heads, middle aged, men and women, boys and more boys, and girls too. And of course mothers had to bring their babies. How many were there? Guess. The number given to me of those who attended the conferences was 28,669. Most of the messages were given by our African brethren. Some too by missionaries.*

> *Much prayer had gone up to the throne of grace. God heard and answered prayer. The Lord was in the midst and the blessed Holy Spirit had control. All messages were given in the tribal language and in Swahili, the trade language of East Africa, translators translating each sentence as it was spoken in one or the other language. Between messages there was a song time by choirs from the main stations, churches and schools. Wish you could have heard all this. Hundreds of people had to sit outside but loudspeakers carried the words to the rear and outside.*

> *In Leviticus 25 where we read, "A jubilee shall the fiftieth be unto you," we also read about the trumpet ministry. We, too, had four African men play the trumpets. The four alone and helping with the congregational singing. A real ministry.*

> *I gave the first address on the morning of August 19th. Much of it historic but not all. People want to know and should know. Only a very few of us old timers are left. And wasn't it wonderful that I could attend this conference 50 years after we first landed at Nassa. The Lord has done great things for us down the years. And to Him all the praise. (12)*

213

**Marie in later years with her good friend Ludia**

## "ALL OF THE NEW AND OLD TESTAMENT"

In 1961, the entire Sukuma Bible came off the press—a 10,000-copy edition. The missionaries who had worked on the original translation—Emil Sywulka and Tom Marsh—were with the Lord by then. But their widows, Margaret Marsh and Marie Sywulka, rejoiced to see the day. Margaret wrote:

> As a copy of the entire Bible in Sukuma was placed in my hands a few days ago, I fled to my room and on my knees poured out my heart full of joy. (13)

When Marie received her copy, tears trickled down her wrinkled cheeks. "My, my," she exclaimed. "To think that after all these years I can hold the Sukuma Bible in my hands." (14)

At eighty-seven, she was celebrating a dream come true—a dream which she and Emil had committed to the Lord more than fifty years before. She sat down and wrote to her grandchildren:

> How good the dear Lord has been to me and to Him all the praise. There are so many things to thank Him for. One

214

*special thing to thank Him for these days is—guess what! The
other day the airmail from England brought us two copies of
the whole Bible in the Sukuma language. More will be sent by
boat, maybe on the way now. We have had the New Testament
for a long time. Also some portions and a few books too of the
Old Testament and now we have in print all of the New and
Old Testament in one book. The whole Bible for the first time!
(15)*

## HAIR RIBBONS AND BANANAS

Two months shy of her 88th birthday, Marie fell, breaking her
right arm and right hip bone. Instead of complaining, she found
reason once again to praise God for His faithfulness:

*The Lord has wonderfully undertaken for me. My general
health is very good. My arm and leg are still off duty. My
twentieth-century wheel chair continues to meet a real need
getting about the house and out of doors. This has been an
expensive affair but "your Father knoweth" and extra funds
have come in to meet every need, from the home and here on
the field—Asian, European and African. The first gift? This
began when a little girl took the ribbons out of her braids and
brought them to me...*

*We have many, many people sick here, even children with
polio. The Lord gave me the privilege of supplying extra food
for them. The Lord made it possible for me to give the sick in
the hospital here a bunch of bananas. (16)*

Amazingly, Marie recovered from both fractures without the
intervention of modern surgery. Soon she was back "on the go,"
attending to guests, giving out Scriptures, and even buying candy
for leprosy patients in Busia. A leaflet from one of her supporting
churches stated: "She does not plan to return to America again,"
and then quoted one of her letters:

*I praise the Lord for His faithfulness and that I am still in His
service in Africa. Be my days many or few I want them to tell
for the Lord Jesus in the salvation of precious souls through
prayer and personal contacts, and through my pen and the
printed page. (17)*

## TANGANYIKA GAINS INDEPENDENCE

In the 1950's and 1960's, people all over colonial Africa were clamoring for independence. Tanganyika was spared much of the bloodshed experienced elsewhere, and a peaceful transition was achieved in 1961 when independence was granted. Marie wrote to her grandchildren:

> *Do you know that at midnight December 9th Tanganyika goes independent? The high officials will be Africans. Some of these men, most of them, have been in high government positions for a long time under the present British government which has certainly done much for Tanganyika. Pray for Tanganyika in these days of need. Pray for all races that are a part of Tanganyika: Africans, Asians and we white people...*
>
> *Especially remember our African Christians in this land here that they will go on with the Lord Jesus Christ, Christ manifested in and through their lives, and that more than ever they will be dependent on their Lord Jesus Christ, spirit, soul and body.*
>
> *I hear that many white people will leave Tanganyika. The [local] people want the missionaries to stay on. "You have done so much for us." How good to know that our times are in His hand, the unfailing God. I feel sure that God will keep these doors open for us. If God be for us, then who can be against us? (18)*

## EDWARD VISITS MARIE

In late 1963, Edward asked his mission for a six-month leave of absence so he could visit his mother. In order to make the most of the trip, he also planned visits to boyhood friends, now missionaries in Kenya.

Edward reached Mwanza in time to celebrate his mother's 90th birthday. Quietly, he tried to assess her situation. She declared most emphatically that she would never leave Tanganyika, but her eyesight was failing and at times she was forgetful. The younger missionaries loved her dearly, called her "Mother Sywulka," and helped her with shopping and banking. But they were concerned about her living alone. Edward wrote to his West Coast relatives:

> *New Years greetings from Mother and me. Mother at ninety*
> *finds it difficult to write and cannot possibly keep up with her*
> *correspondence. As you know her eyesight has been failing*
> *during the last year... so it is my privilege to help her out in*
> *many little ways while I am here...*
>
> *Miss Tilley, who lives just across the street, and who has been*
> *a close friend of Mother's for some 35 years here in*
> *Tanganyika, had us out to dinner four or five times... These*
> *changes are good for Mother. (19)*

## THE FIELD COUNCIL'S DECISION

Edward did not want to mention a possible change to his mother until after the Field Council met. In Kenya, where he had gone to visit his friend Raymond Stauffacher, he received a letter from the AIM's Mr. Stier:

> *The Field Council decided that Mother Sywulka should return*
> *to the States. I feel quite sure this is of the Lord taking all*
> *things into consideration. I spoke to her Thursday morning.*
> *She took it very well, as a good soldier of Jesus Christ. We*
> *should pray for her as the thought of it has time to sink in. (20)*

And so Edward returned to Mwanza and made reservations for a May 12, 1964, flight to New York. He explained his plans in a letter to Pauline:

> *From New York I am planning to take Mother straight on to*
> *Akron, as it will likely be her only chance to see the loved ones*
> *there. Also the thought of seeing them, especially Uncle Adam,*
> *should be an incentive to her to make the trip. That will give*
> *us a week or so before flying to Media. (21)*

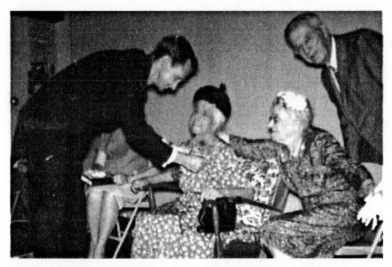

**Marie (left center) with Akron relatives - 1964**

## *COMING FULL CIRCLE*

Somewhat reluctantly, Marie boarded the airplane for her first flight ever. Remembering her forty-day sea voyages from long ago, she must have marveled at how quickly she and Edward crossed the ocean by air.

Her visit to Akron, her girlhood home, brought her around full circle. Of her original family, only she—the eldest—and her brother Adam—the youngest—remained. But there were nieces and nephews, and grand-nieces and grand-nephews, in abundance. Here she was treated as something of a celebrity; the local newspaper even sent a reporter to take her picture and do a feature article about her.

Marie's home church, now called Calvary Evangelical United Brethren, promised to keep on sending $40.00 a month through the AIM. And her cousin Phil Herwig planned to continue his monthly $10.00 gifts. Her retirement needs would be met. Edward wrote: "Mother has a good supply of clothing at present, and her needs are few and simple at Media. If I know her, she will not be spending much." (22)

**Akron relatives. In front are Adam Snyder, Marie, Edward**

## *"I MISS MY AFRICA, BUT GOD IS FAITHFUL"*

From Akron, Edward took his mother to "Media," the lovely AIM retirement home in Florida. There she was close to old and dear friends. Margaret Marsh, especially, counted it a privilege to minister to Marie as needs arose.

**Retirees at Media. Marie is third from left.**

Intercession became Marie's primary ministry in Florida. She prayed for each of her loved ones by name, and also prayed "around the world" for the many missionaries she knew.

Marie's life-long habit of praising the Lord now stood her in good stead as she made the adjustment. From her new home, she wrote to her grandson Paul Emil:

> *As always, I was so glad to hear from you. As you know we have three Paul Sywulkas: Your uncle in Wheaton, his son Paul Andrew and you. Other Paul relatives too. Paul Baumert, my nephew in Easton Pennsylvania... All of the dear relatives are remembered at the throne of grace. And here I am down in Florida and the dear Lord cares for me more than I can tell. To Him all the praise...*
>
> *I do miss my beloved Africa, country and people. I landed in Africa for the first time in July 1906. Miss Snyder then. I have never regretted having answered God's call for service in Africa. I carried on the dispensary work down the years where we lived in various places in Africa. Am not doing anything along that line now and miss it. Don't need to here. My household belongings, furniture, dishes, and much else is*

220

*being sold and I will receive money for the same in due time.*
*This will help pay my expenses here for room, food, etc...*

*I had a great and lovely surprise two days ago. A sister of*
*Emil's sent me a check for $100! The Lord reward her. I know*
*He will. This will help meet my expenses here. $30.00 a month*
*for room, meals, and then there are other expenses too. God is*
*faithful. (23)*

Marie remained at Media for seven more years, enjoying good care, warm fellowship, and occasional visits from college-age grandchildren. As she grew increasingly forgetful, she often repeated herself. But the phrases she repeated were all full of praise: "I have two graves in Africa, but no regrets." "I miss my Africa, but I thank God for this beautiful place." And always, "God is faithful."

**Marie in Florida, with grandson Steve and his wife Elisa**

## *AND SO SHE PASSED OVER*

On June 22, 1971, Marie passed away peacefully at ninety-seven and a half years of age. Her son Paul was the only blood relative at the memorial service, but her AIM family was well represented. Fellow missionary Laura Thompson wrote:

> *I wish I could say how much Mother Sywulka meant to me personally and to all the AIM family in Tanzania. It was through her husband that I was called to the field. There they received me and loved and prayed for me through many years. What an inspiration dear Mrs. Sywulka was to me in her loving, sacrificial service to the Lord, to the Africans who were so dear to her, and to her fellow missionaries and others who crossed her path. I'm sure many Africans, as well as others, were in the ransomed throng that received her.*
>
> *Now she has seen our Lord face to face and her dear ones whom she had "lost awhile."*

"And Christ, her Lord and Master, the One her soul adored,
 For whose dear sake she labored, is now her great reward;
  Forever shall she serve Him, forever see His face—
And the trumpets all are sounding the glories of His grace."

*"So he passed over (Mr. Valiant for the Truth) and all the trumpets sounded for him on the other side." (24)*

**References:**

(1) Letter from Marie to Edward and Pauline, Aug. 22, 1949
(2) Circular from Edward and Pauline Sywulka, Nov. 1, 1950
(3) Letter from Marie to Edward and Pauline, Aug. 13, 1950
(4) Sywulka, *Workers together with Him,* introduction
(5) *Ibid*, p. 23
(6) *Ibid*, p. 32
(7) Letter from Marie to Edward and Pauline, Nov. 30, 1952
(8) *Inland Africa,* "Mrs. Emil Sywulka completes fifty years of service," by Nellie Stover
(9) *Ibid.*
(10) *South of Victoria,* June 1960, "Press Dedication follows year of prayer"
(11) *South of Victoria,* June 1960, "Converging to one point"
(12) Letter from Marie to granddaughter Anna Marie, Sept. 12, 1959
(13) Wadell, Genny, *Safari Servant,* p. 120.
(14) Anderson, Dick, *We felt like grasshoppers,* p. 56
(15) Letter from Marie to Anna Marie, Paul, Stephen and Dora Sywulka, April 26, 1961
(16) Circular from Marie, 1961
(17) Missionary picture leaflet from a supporting church, undated
(18) Letter from Marie to Anna Marie and Stephen Sywulka, Nov. 29, 1961
(19) Letter from Edward to "Family on the West Coast," Feb. 10, 1964
(20) Letter from Mr. Stier to Edward, quoted in a letter from Edward to Pauline, April 2, 1964
(21) Letter from Edward to Pauline, April 2, 1964
(22) Letter from Edward to "Relatives," July 16, 1964
(23) Letter from Marie to grandson Paul Emil, July 4, 1964
(24) Thompson, Laura, "A tribute: Mrs. Emil Sywulka," *Inland Africa,* 1971

Printed in the United States
25199LVS00003B/301-333